2012 ROMAN REPLIES & CLSA ADVISORY OPINIONS

SR. SHARON A. EUART, RSM, JCD
EDITOR, ROMAN REPLIES

REV. MSGR. JOHN A. ALESANDRO, JCD, JD
REV. MSGR. THOMAS J. GREEN, JCD
EDITORS, ADVISORY OPINIONS

Canon Law Society of America

ISBN 1-932208-33-X
ISSN 1543-4230
SAN 237-6296

Unless otherwise noted, all canons quoted are from the *Code of Canon Law, Latin-English Edition* (Washington, DC: Canon Law Society of America, 1999) and the *Code of Canons of the Eastern Churches, Latin-English Edition* (Washington, DC: Canon Law Society of America, 2002).

Printed in the United States of America.

Canon Law Society of America
Office of the Executive Coordinator
The Hecker Center, Suite 111
3025 Fourth Street, NE
Washington, DC 20017-1102

Table Of Contents

OTHER DOCUMENTS

ADVISORY OPINIONS 2012

CODE OF CANON LAW

FOREWORD

The Canon Law Society of America (CLSA) publishes annually *Roman Replies and CLSA Advisory Opinions* for canonists and those seeking a clearer understanding of the *praxis legis* of the Catholic Church. The combination of these two services, begun in 1984, continues to serve as useful resources for those involved in the application of canonical discipline.

The compilation of materials for *Roman Replies 2012* was guided by Sister Sharon A. Euart, RSM, CLSA Executive Coordinator. The collection of entries in this issue, when viewed in conjunction with previous volumes, assists the reader both in understanding recent developments in the law and in identifying current trends in the praxis of the Roman Curia.

The selection and assembly of opinions for *CLSA Advisory Opinions 2012* was provided by the CLSA Publications Advisory Board, chaired by Monsignor John A. Alesandro. The topics addressed in the opinions reflect a variety of canonical issues and demonstrate the scope of canonical expertise and reflection by members of the Society. Editorial assistance was provided by Amy Tadlock, Administrative Assistant, Office of the Executive Coordinator.

Roman Replies and CLSA Advisory Opinions that are out-of-print are available electronically on the CLSA website (www.clsa.org).

The CLSA provides this series as a professional resource. Care should be taken in considering the relative weight of the materials found in this publication. The principles for canonical interpretation (*CIC* cc. 16-19 and *CCEO* cc. 1498-1501) serve as guides in considering the contents of this volume.

Sister Sharon A. Euart, RSM, JCD
Executive Coordinator

Roman Replies

Introductory Note

The following is the editorial policy of Roman Replies. The policy, as well as the source of these materials, was first described in the 1984 edition and, with some modifications, has been in effect since that time.

Each year members of the Canon Law Society of America are invited to submit recent replies from the various dicasteries of the Holy See which might be of interest to the Society's members and the wider church. Judicial vicars, chancellors, vicars general, major superiors of institutes of consecrated life and societies of apostolic life in the United States, and professors of canon law are encouraged and asked to submit material for this important publication.

Contributions from members of the Society resident in other countries or members of other canon law societies are always most welcome. All contributors receive a complimentary copy of the volume.

Certain editorial principles determine the selection of documents for this publication. First, in general, entries which have already appeared in various canonical journals would not normally be repeated here. An exception is the publication of an official English translation of documents which already has been published in an unofficial translation. Second, documents which merely restate something published earlier with no added nuances or changes are not normally included. Third, documents that concern a matter not yet resolved by the Roman dicasteries are held for future publication in the hope that the entire matter may be fully reported when the question or controversy has been resolved. Finally, all details of names and places are changed to protect confidentiality, unless otherwise specified by the submitting individual.

A special note of thanks to all those who have submitted texts, helped with translations and who otherwise contributed to this 2012 edition. It is our hope that this volume continues to be a service to all who work in the ministry of justice in the Church.

Contributions may be sent to:

Canon Law Society of America
Office of the Executive Coordinator
3025 Fourth Street, NE
The Hecker Center, Suite 111
Washington, DC 20017-1102

CANONS 50, 127 §2, 515 §2 AND 1222 §2

SUPREESSION OF A PARISH AND CLOSURE OF A PARISH CHURCH

A diocesan bishop, continuing a study of the diocese initiated by his predecessor and considering the study's broad trends, closed and merged parishes within the diocese. In many of these parish closings and mergers, the parish church was also closed and the buildings locked. Parishioners made hierarchical recourse to the Congregation for the Clergy regarding the suppression of the parish (c. 515 §2) and the closure of the church (c. 1222 §2). Below is the Congregation's response.

CONGREGATIO PRO CLERICIS
Prot. No. ______

DECREE

1. Whereas the Bishop Emeritus of ______, United States of America, the Most Reverend ______, initiated a pastoral planning process entitled ______, to study the vibrancy of parish communities, and possible sharing of resources among those parishes;
2. Whereas the Most Reverend ______, after his appointment as Bishop of ______ in 2006, continued this study, in conformity with Canon 50 of the Code of Canon law; this same pastoral planning process had considered broad diocesan trends concerning the situation of the declining number of the clergy and the ratio of priests to Catholic faithful, the general location of parish communities and churches, weekly attendance at Sunday Mass, finances, with a special emphasis on the vibrancy of the parish communities, judged by the above and other predetermined factors;
3. Whereas in many of the parish "closings" and mergers within the Diocese, the parish Church was also closed and it was declared that Holy Mass and devotional visits were never again to take place within those edifices, those edifices in all instances being locked and in some instances being fenced off;
4. Whereas the Bishop of ______ was advised on several occasions that proce-

dures leading to the possible merger of a parish (c. 515 §2) would not *ipso iure* enable him perpetually to close a Church to divine worship and the devotion of the faithful, His Excellency being invited to revisit his procedure to remedy any possible invalidating defects, but declining to do so;

5. Whereas the process included an examination of the possible "closing" of the Parish of ______, a territorial parish in the ______ section of ______;

6. Whereas on 3 February 2009, with a stated view of fulfilling the requirements of c. 515 §2, the Diocesan Bishop heard the opinions of the members of the Presbyteral Council regarding the proposal with relation to ______ Parish and other parishes in the cluster, with no definite solution proposed;

7. Whereas on 12 March 2009, by letter to the pastor and subsequent announcement in the Church, the Diocesan Bishop communicated his decision to "close" and merge ______ Parish, stating that he would decide afterward whether ______ Church would be chosen as the "worship site" of the new parish;

8. Whereas on 20 March 2009, Ms. ______ made written requests to the Diocesan Bishop to amend his decree, asking in her letter that ______ be allowed to remain open as a "stand alone" parish, rather than be merged;

9. Whereas on 21 April 2009, the Bishop of ______ replied in the negative to the request that he change his disposition in the matter;

10. Whereas on 26 April 2009, Ms. ______ made hierarchical recourse to the Congregation for the Clergy, within the canonical time limits;

11. Whereas on 27 May 2009, the Bishop wrote to Fr. ______, Pastor of ______ Parish, notifying him that he had decided that, in the merger of the parish, an alternate edifice would remain the "worship site," indicating also that the Catholic School located on the parish grounds would continue, as well as the cemetery adjacent to the Church, but ______ Church itself would be unable to be used for any function of Worship, thereby executing the provisions of c. 1222 §2 without implementing its procedures;

12. Whereas on 1 June 2009 the Pastor replied to the Bishop of ______, asking for a reconsideration of this disposition, and on 9 June 2009, a group of parishioners, headed by Ms. ______, also wrote to the Bishop to request that he modify his dispositions;

13. Whereas on 2 July 2009, at a meeting with Bishop ______, he indicated to

recurrents that he refused to modify his dispositions, replying to them by letter on 7 July 2009;

14. Whereas on 2 July 2009, this group of recurrents, headed by Ms. ______, which is now making recourse in concert with Ms. ______ and represented by Avv. ______, made hierarchical recourse to the Congregation for the Clergy, the Dicastery by reason of connection issuing one decree to respond to all;

15. Whereas the Bishop of ______, in his letter to this Dicastery of 6 July 2009 (Prot. N. ______) stated that the appeal against his disposition was invalid, because the recurrents chose to appeal after his 27 May letter, rather than after his 12 March letter, and so lost their right to appeal in March;

16. Whereas the Congregation replied to the Bishop, by letter of 8 September 2009 (Prot. N. ______), stating that the presentation of the hierarchical recourse was considered valid and the study was ongoing;

17. Whereas, although the Bishop of ______ submitted the acts of the case, and the parish celebrated the last parish Sunday Mass in June of 2010, no decree was submitted, the Congregation, then, takes as an indication of His Excellency's dispositions the 12 March 2009 and the 27 May 2009 letters to the pastor of St. ______, both of which were co-signed by Sister ______, Chancellor.

18. An Hierarchical Recourse is by its nature a documentary process which proceeds on the basis of examination of authentic documents provided by interested parties at the request of the Dicastery: thus, having provided ample opportunity for all interested parties to respond, the Dicastery judges as complete the documentation in its possession and proceeds therefore to its decision *per cartas*;

19. The law requires for validity that the Diocesan Bishop consult the Presbyteral Council in order to seek the advice of its members before coming to his decision regarding the suppression of a parish (cf. c. 127 §2 and c. 515 §2). Finally, a legitimate decree should be issued, stating at least in a summary fashion the lawful motivations supporting the decision (cf. c. 51), formalizing the Bishop's decision and making them manifest to those who have interests in the matter.

20. In this matter, the Bishop of ______ was given sufficient time to present to this Dicastery information which would solidify the decisions he made, and

to forward all of the acts pertinent in the matter to the Congregation. The absence of any decree indicating and formalizing the dispositions of the Bishop made in the letter of 12 March 2009 and 27 May 2009 is troubling. Even should this document be taken as a manifestation of the Bishop's dispositions in the matter, which is the essence of a decree, it can be clearly seen that it lacks the requisite elements indicated by the canons. Hence, the Bishop of ______ is held to have acted in violation of the law on procedural grounds with regard to c. 515 §2.

21. Regarding relegation of ______ Church to secular but not unbecoming use, it is noted that the Bishop's letter of 27 May 2009 omits any specific reference to the relegation of the church to secular but not unbecoming use, or to the canonical process required by c. 1222 §2. It is apparent from the acts, however, that the Diocesan Bishop did in fact arrive at a decision to implement the effects of the process envisioned by c. 1222 §2 without fulfilling its procedures. The Bishop's letter to the pastor of 27 May 2009 is quite specific, indicating that the Church would not be used after the merger of the parish. In doing so, an essential element for the validity of the relegation of a church to secular but not unbecoming use was omitted, i.e., the required consultation of the Presbyteral Council regarding the matter (cf. c. 127 §2 and c. 1222 §2). The Bishop of ______, even after being advised as to these shortfalls by the Congregation's letter of 8 September 2009 (Prot. No. ______) declined to clarify the matter either by allowing the Church to remain open for divine worship and the devotion of the faithful, or by following the procedure for relegation. By the law itself, such an omission renders invalid the Bishop's decision to implement the effects of c. 1222 §2, i.e., the permanent closure of ______ Church and its concomitant relegation to secular but not unbecoming use.

22. Jurisprudence does not recognize such relegation to be implicit in the decree suppressing or amalgamating a parish (cf. Decree of the Supreme Tribunal of the Apostolic Signatura of 1 July 2010, par. 7: "*Iurisprudentia Signaturae Apostolicae negat reductionem ecclesiae implicite statui posse in decreto suppressionis paroeciae.*" Prot. no. ______). It is evident, therefore, that the requirements of the law for the licit and valid relegation of a church to secular but not unbecoming use have not been met, and that ______ Church has not been lawfully and validly relegated to secular but not unbecoming use. Therefore:

The Congregation hereby decrees that this petition for recourse as presented, with regard to the suppression of ______ Parish (c. 515 §2) does have canonical basis in law and in fact, and so is upheld both *de procedendo* and *de decernendo.*

The Congregation further decrees that this petition for recourse as presented, with regard to the closure of ______ Church (c. 1222 §2) does have canonical basis in law and in fact, and so is upheld both *de procedendo* and *de decernendo.*

The Bishop of ______ is instructed to enact the implications of this Decree.

Recourse against this Decree may be made before the Supreme Tribunal of the Apostolic Signatura within the peremptory time limits established in the Apostolic Letter *motu proprio Antiqua Ordinatione*, Art. 34 §1.

(signed)
Mauro Cardinal Piacenza
Prefect

(signed)
+Celso Morga Iruzubieta
Titular Archbishop of Alba marittima
Secretary

Given at the Seat of the Congregation for the Clergy
1 March 2012

Canon 181

Postulation

This reply from an Undersecretary of the Congregation for Institutes of Consecrated Life and Societies of Apostolic Life indicates that the Congregation "expects" a candidate who needs postulation to receive the two-thirds majority on the first or second ballot or he/she loses passive voice on subsequent ballots. This restriction is not in the Code of Canon Law, and the religious institute in question has a maximum of four ballots for provincial superior. The provision would obtain the force of law (ius), however, by its inclusion in the Constitutions as demanded by the Congregation.

Vatican City
June 2, 2012

Prot. S. 48-1/2008

Reverend Father,

In reference to the information you request in your letter of May 7, I would like to inform you of the Congregation's practice. We expect a candidate who needs postulation for an office to receive a qualified majority of two-thirds of the votes on the first or second ballot.

This practice should be included in your Constitutions for cases that require postulation. Therefore, after a second inconclusive ballot (two-thirds majority is not achieved), there should be a new ballot in which the previous candidate loses his passive voice....

Please accept our warm greetings and best wishes for each of your friars.

(signed)
Father Sebastiano Paciolla, O.Cist.
Undersecretary

CANON 220

PSYCHOLOGICAL EVALUATIONS AND THE RIGHT TO PRIVACY

In a petition for a dispensation from the obligations of Holy Orders for a priest, a Diocesan Bishop raised a question with the Congregation for the Clergy concerning psychological evaluations and the right the privacy. The Congregation's response follows.

CONGREGATION FOR THE CLERGY
July 12, 2012
Prot. N. ______

Your Excellency,

This Congregation has received and thanks Your Excellency for your letter of ______, together with the petition and related documentation for the dispensation from the obligations of Holy Orders on behalf of the Rev. ______. The formal acknowledgement of the Dicastery is enclosed herewith.

With regard to the question Your Excellency raises concerning psychological evaluations and the right to privacy, this Congregation continues to hold that a priest is under no obligation to disclose the full contents of such reports, but may choose to do so. However, any diagnosis should be disclosed to the Ordinary, as this may relate directly to the fitness and suitability of the priest for ministry in general or for particular types of ministry.

In many cases, an Ordinary may be in possession of a full psychological evaluation. In such instances, this Dicastery is pleased to receive a copy as it can be of value in the assessment of the matter before it.

I avail of this opportunity to renew my sentiments of esteem and with every best wish, I remain,

Sincerely yours in Christ,

(Signed)
+Celso Morga Iruzubieta
Titular Archbishop of Alba marittima
Secretary

Canon 277 §1

Married Permanent Deacons and Observance of Perfect and Perpetual Continence

The President of the United States Conference of Catholic Bishops, at the request of the USCCB Committee on Clergy, Consecrated Life and Vocations and the Committee on Canonical Affairs and Church Governance, sought a clarification from the Pontifical Council for Legislative Texts on the observance of diaconal continence by married deacons in the Latin Catholic Church. The observation of the President and Secretary of the Pontifical Council, which were formulated in consultation with the Congregation for the Doctrine of the Faith, clarify that married permanent deacons are not bound to observe perfect and perpetual continence, as long as their marriage lasts. The Pontifical Council's response follows.

PONTIFICAL COUNCIL FOR LEGISLATIVE TEXTS
December 17, 2011
Prot. 13095/2011

Your Excellency:

I refer to your letter of April 8, 2011 in which Your Excellency has requested this Pontifical Council to clarify whether married permanent deacons, so long as their marriage lasts, are bound to observe the perfect and perpetual continence indicated by can. 277, §1 CIC. The question was raised because some have expressed the opinion that permanent deacons are also bound to the obligation which the said canon imposes on clerics in general.

It should be noted that often the canonical discipline on a given topic is not inferred from the wording of a single legal precept, but rather from the whole set of existing regulation on the matter in the law of the Church, always in harmony with what has been stated by the Church's Magisterium. This is what can. 17 CIC prescribes.

With regard specifically to the question above, after consultation with the Congregation for the Doctrine of the Faith and having made the necessary studies, this Pontifical Council offers the following observations.

1. In can. 277, §3 CIC, the requirement of perfect and perpetual continence is inseparably linked to the obligation of celibacy to which all clerics, in principle, are bound.

Also can. 1037 CIC requires that unmarried candidates for the permanent diaconate must assume the obligation of celibacy prior to ordination. Furthermore, can. 1087 CIC establishes an impediment to marriage for those in sacred orders. For this reason, permanent deacons who are widowers cannot marry, unless being dispensed, and therefore are bound to observe perfect and perpetual continence.

The particular discipline of these last two canons, 1037 and 1087 CIC, applicable to certain situations of permanent deacons, explains on the one hand why can. 288 CIC did not exempt in a general way "all" permanent deacons from the obligation of continence established by the can. 277, §1 CIC; and on the other hand how it is evident from all these norms that the canon wanted to exempt married permanent deacons from such obligation of continence so long as their marriage lasts.

2. Indeed, can. 1031, §2 CIC admits married men to the clerical state in the particular cases of permanent deacons, but states nothing about a hypothetical obligation to observe perfect and perpetual continence, as the Legislator would indicate if such an obligation were to be established.

Ultimately, the fact that in order for a married man to be admitted to the Order of the diaconate, the consent of his wife is required (cfr. Can. 1031, §2 CIC) implies that an explicit consent would have been required for reasons of justice if the condition of permanent deacon had entailed the obligation of perfect and perpetual continence (cfr. Can. 1055 CIC).

3. Naturally, this canonical discipline does not state anything apart from what the Church's Magisterium has already affirmed in this regard. In fact, the Dogmatic Constitution *Lumen gentium*, n. 29 (§2), and other successive normative documents of the Holy See, appear to take for granted that married permanent deacons live their marriage in the ordinary way (cfr., above all, CONGREGATIO DE INSTITUTIONE CATHOLICA *Ratio fundamentalis institutionis diaconorum permanentium, Instituto diaconorum* of February 22, 1998 (nn. 7, 27, 33, 45, 50, 59-62, and particularly n. 61).

In conclusion, the current canonical discipline does not require married permanent deacons, so long as their marriage lasts, to observe the obligation of perfect and perpetual continence established by can. 277, §1 CIC for clerics in general.

I hope that these clarifications, briefly presented in this letter, may be helpful to Your Excellency in indicating what the content of the canonical discipline is at this point.

While remaining at your disposal for any further clarifications, I take this opportunity to extend to you and the members of your Conference my sentiments of personal esteem and prayerful best wishes for a Blessed Christmas and a fruitful New Year.

Sincerely yours in Christ,

(signed)
+Francesco Coccopalmerio
President

(signed)
+Juan Ignacio Arrieta
Secretary

Canon 290

Dispensation from the Obligations of Ordination

A Diocesan Bishop requested from the Holy Father a dispensation from the obligations of Holy Orders for a priest who had left the active ministry and who was seriously ill and in danger of death. The Congregation for the Clergy granted the requested favor in virtue of the special faculty granted by Pope Benedict XVI in August 2005. The rescript of the Congregation follows.

CONGREGATION FOR THE CLERGY

Prot. N. ________

Most Holy Father

_____, priest of the diocese of _____, having left active ministry, and seriously ill and in mortal danger, humbly requests from Your Holiness the dispensation from obligations from Holy Orders (and flowing from religious vows) in order to be reconciled with the God and the Church, so that he can seek his heavenly homeland.

CONGREGATION FOR THE CLERGY

on the 4th day of June 2012

in virtue of the special faculty granted by the Supreme Pontiff Benedict XVI (Secr. St. N. 907, August 10, 2005), and by his special mandate, in consideration of the gravity of the case and circumstances presented in his request and the opinion of his Ordinary, kindly grants the requested favor as follows:

1. The rescript takes effect immediately when it is made known to him.

2. The competent Ordinary is to make known the rescript of the dispensation as quickly as possible. It includes inseparably the dispensation from priestly celibacy as well as the loss of the clerical state. It is never lawful for the petitioner to separate these two elements, i.e., to accept the first and to refuse the second. If the petitioner is a religious, the rescript also concedes a dispensation from vows. In addition, it also includes absolution from censures, if such is needed.

3. Notice of the grant of dispensation should be recorded in the baptismal register of the petitioner's parish of baptism.

4. With regard to the canonical celebration of marriage, the norms laid down in the *Code of Canon Law* are to be applied. But the Ordinary should see to it that such arrangements are carried out with caution and without pomp or outward display.

5. If the petitioner ceases to be in immanent danger of death, the ecclesiastical authority, whose task it is to notify the petitioner, will exhort him to participate in the life of the People of God in accord with his new condition of life, and give edification and conduct himself as an upright son of the Church. At the same time the Ordinary will make the following known to him:

a) The dispensed priest automatically loses all the rights proper to the clerical state, dignities and offices; he is no longer obliged by the other obligations connected with the clerical state.

b) He is excluded from the exercise of sacred ministry, except those in canons 976 and 986 §2[1] and for that reason he is not permitted to give a homily, nor can he exercise a position of pastoral authority or parish administration.

c) Likewise he cannot exercise any office in seminaries or equivalent institutions. In other institutions of higher studies in any way depending on ecclesiastical authority, he cannot have a position of authority.

d) In institutes of higher studies not depending on ecclesiastical authority, he cannot teach properly theological disciplines or those closely connected.

e) In institutions of lower studies depending on ecclesiastical authority, he cannot hold a position of authority or the office of teaching a properly theological discipline. A dispensed priest is obliged by the same law concerning teaching religion in institutes of this type which do not depend on ecclesiastical authority;

f) Per se, a priest dispensed from priestly celibacy and *a fortiori* joined in marriage ought to absent himself from the place in which his former condition is known; nor is he able to perform anywhere the function of lector or acolyte or distribute Eucharistic communion.

1 Can. 976. Even though a priest lacks the faculty to hear confessions, he absolves validly and licitly any penitents whatsoever in danger of death from any censures and sins, even if an approved priest is present. Can. 986 §2. In urgent necessity, any confessor is obliged to hear the confessions of the Christian faithful, and in danger of death, any priest is so obliged.

6. The Ordinary of the domicile or the place where the petitioner is staying, according to his prudent and conscientious judgment, having heard any interested parties and reflecting carefully on the circumstances, can dispense from any and all clauses of the rescript under letters **e** and **f**.

7. As a rule, these dispensations should be given only after a period of time from the notification of the loss of the clerical state has been granted, and they be given in writing.

8. Lastly, some work of piety or charity should be imposed on the petitioner.

9. At an opportune time, the competent Ordinary should report to this Congregation briefly about the notification having been accomplished, and, if there might be any wonderment on the part of the faithful, a prudent explanation should be provided.

All other contrary provisions notwithstanding.
From the office of the Congregation, on the 4th day of June 2012.

(signed)
Mauro Card. Picenza
Prefect

(signed)
+Celso Morga Iruzubieta
Archbishop Secretary

Canon 290 and Special Faculties for the Congregation for the Clergy Administrative Procedure for Laicization of Priests

Loss of the Clerical State and Dispensation from Sacred Celibacy and All the Obligations Connected with Sacred Ordination

In 2009 Pope Benedict XVI granted the Congregation for the Clergy three special faculties for dismissal of clerics from the priesthood and the obligations of celibacy in certain circumstances. The following case was submitted to the Congregation for the Clergy as an application of the third of the special faculties granted by Pope Benedict XVI. The rescript from the Congregation follows.

CONGREGATION FOR THE CLERGY
Prot. N. ____

His Excellency, Bishop of ________, humbly petitions the declaration of loss of the clerical state and the dispensation from sacred celibacy and from all the obligations connected with sacred ordination for Mr.__ belonging to the same [arch]diocese.

May 31, 2012

The instruction has been completed and everything required has been done, the petition is accepted and the loss of the clerical state is granted to the aforementioned priest by a supreme and unappealable decision that is not subject to recourse.

The dispensation from sacred celibacy and from all the obligations connected to holy orders is also granted to the same priest according to the following reasons:

1. The loss and dispensation take effect from the moment of mentioned decision.

2. The competent Ordinary of the place will inform the priest of the rescript of the loss and dispensation; these two can never be separated. In addition to this, the rescript includes the absolution of censures insofar as this is necessary.

3. Annotation of the loss and dispensation will be made in the baptismal register of the parish of the same priest.

4. With regard to the canonical celebration of marriage, if this is to take place, the norms laid down in the Code of Canon Law are to be applied; the Ordinary should see to it that such arrangements are carried out with caution and without outward display.

5. The ecclesiastical authority whose responsibility it is to communicate the rescript to the petitioner should earnestly exhort him to participate in the life of the People of God in a manner which is in harmony with his new condition in life, that he give good example, and thus show himself to be an upright son of the Church. But at the same time, he should take note of those things which follow:

a) The dispensed priest is also relieved of all rights proper to the clerical state, and dignities and ecclesiastical offices connected with the clerical state; he is no longer bound by the other obligations of the clerical state;

b) he remains excluded from the exercise of the sacred ministry, with the exceptions mentioned in canons 976 and 986, §2 of the Code of Canon Law, and therefore may not give a homily. Nor is he able to exercise a supervisory office in the pastoral sphere, or perform the function of parochial administrator;

c) he likewise cannot perform any function in seminaries and equivalent institutions. In other institutions of higher studies, which depend in any manner whatsoever upon ecclesiastical authority, he cannot exercise a supervisory position or a teaching post;

d) in other institutions of higher studies which do not depend upon ecclesiastical authority, he cannot teach any theological discipline;

e) in institutions of lower studies which depend upon ecclesiastical authority, he cannot discharge a supervisory position or teacher. A dispensed priest is bound by the same law concerning teaching religion in institutions of this type which do not depend on ecclesiastical authority;

6. The Ordinary will see to it, insofar as possible, that the new condition of the priest is not an occasion of scandal to the faithful.

7. Concerning the notification of the loss [of the clerical state] and dispensation, the present document will be read to the priest by a notary or ecclesiastical actuary, and will be signed by both.

8. At a proper and opportune time, the competent Ordinary must send a copy

of the rescript signed by the priest recognizing his reception and acceptance of this rescript and also of the restrictions. If this is not done, the whole effect of the rescript remains. Then he will send to the Congregation a report of the notification and provide a prudent explanation if there was admiration of the faithful.

9. The Chancellor of the competent curia will draw up and sign a receipt of this rescript if the priest so desires and give it to him for his use.

All contrary provisions notwithstanding.

From the office of the Congregation, on the 12th day of June, 2012

(signed)
Maurus Card. Picenza
Prefect

(signed)
+Celsus Morga Iruzubieta
Titular Archbishop of Alba marittima
Secretary

CANON 638 §3

REQUEST FOR A DEBT CEILING

A Superior General of a religious institute that sponsors a Catholic Health System in the United States wrote to the Congregation for Institutes of Consecrated Life and Societies of Apostolic Life requesting a debt ceiling rather than having to request separate indults for individual loans. The Congregation's response follows.

CONGREGATION FOR INSTITUTES OF CONSECRATED LIFE AND SOCIETIES OF APOSTOLIC LIFE

20 April 2012
Prot. N.______

Dear ______,

We have received your fax of 9 March 2012, in which you enquire about the process by which a religious institute with a large health care system might receive permission from this Dicastery for a debt ceiling, instead of asking for separate indults for individual loans.

This permission is not granted often. If there is a particular need, the Superior General of the Institute concerned should present a petition to the Dicastery, including the reasons for the petition, the extract from the minutes of the Council meeting at which the consent of the Council was obtained, a summary financial statement of the whole system for the past few years, including the current state of indebtedness and an opinion from an independent expert on the capacity of the system to service the additional debt. The petition should also mention any previously granted indults for loans in the recent past.

In any case, if an institute were to consider such a petition, we recommend they write to us for information.

With sincere good wishes in the Lord,

(signed)
Sr. Nicoletta V. Spezzati, A.S.C.
Undersecretary

CANONS 708 AND 709

DOCTRINAL ASSESSMENT OF THE LEADERSHIP CONFERENCE OF WOMEN RELIGIOUS

In April 2008 the Congregation for the Doctine of the Faith initiated a doctrinal assessment of the Leadership Conference of Women Religious (LCWR) in the United States. In April 2012 the findings of the assessment were presented to the leadership of LCWR by the Congregation and made public. The statement of Cardinal William Levada, Prefect, and the report of the findings follows.

Statement of Cardinal William Levada, Prefect of the Congregation for the Doctrine of the Faith, on the Doctrinal Assessment of the LCWR

The findings of the doctrinal Assessment of the Leadership Conference of Women Religious (LCWR) released today by the Congregation for the Doctrine of the Faith are aimed at fostering a patient and collaborative renewal of this conference of major superiors in order to provide a stronger doctrinal foundation for its many laudable initiatives and activities.

The first step in the implementation of the findings of the doctrinal Assessment consists, therefore, in a personal meeting between the Superiors of the Congregation for the Doctrine of the Faith and the Officers of the LCWR. Such a personal encounter allows for the opportunity to review the document together in a spirit of mutual respect and collaboration, hopefully thereby avoiding possible misunderstandings of the document's intent and scope. In this sense, I also express my gratitude to the Officers of the LCWR for their openness and participation in the doctrinal Assessment since 2008 when I first communicated to them the Congregation's intention to undertake this project.

In his Apostolic Letter *Porta Fidei* announcing the Year of Faith which will begin in October, 2012, Pope Benedict XVI reminds us that it is the Church's faith that sustains and animates Christian life and witness: *"The renewal of the Church is also achieved through the witness offered by the lives of believers: by their very existence in the world, Christians are called to radiate the word of truth that the Lord Jesus has left us.*"[1] This is all the more true for those who offer the Church and the world the most eloquent witness of religious consecration.

As the issues evidenced in the doctrinal Assessment involve essential questions of faith, the Holy Father has given the Congregation for the Doctrine of the Faith a special mandate to collaborate with the LCWR in a renewal of their work through a concentrated reflection on the doctrinal foundations of that work. This process will necessarily involve communication and coordination with the United States Conference of Catholic Bishops, the Congregation for Institutes of Consecrated Life and Societies of Apostolic Life, and the Congregation for Bishops.

The overarching aim of the doctrinal Assessment is, therefore, to assist the LCWR in the United States in implementing an ecclesiology of communion, confident that "*the joyous rediscovery of faith can also contribute to consolidate the unity and communion among the different bodies that make up the wider family of the Church.*"[2]

CONGREGATIO PRO DOCTRINA FIDEI

Doctrinal Assessment of the Leadership Conference of Women Religious

I. Introduction

The context in which the current doctrinal Assessment of the Leadership Conference of Women Religious in the United States of America is best situated is articulated by Pope John Paul II in the Post-Synodal Apostolic Exhortation *Vita consecrata* of 1996. Commenting on the genius of the charism of religious life in the Church, Pope John Paul says: "*In founders and foundresses we see a constant and lively sense of the Church, which they manifest by their full participation in all aspects of the Church's life, and in their ready obedience to the Bishops and especially to the Roman Pontiff. Against this background of love towards Holy Church 'the pillar and bulwark of truth' (1 Tim 3:15), we readily understand... the full ecclesial communion which the Saints, founders and foundresses, have shared in diverse and often difficult times and circumstances. They are examples which consecrated persons need constantly to recall if they are to resist the par-*

1 Pope Benedixt XVI, Apostolic Letter *Porta Fidei*, no. 6.

2 Congregation for the Doctrine of the Faith, *Note with pastoral recommendations for the Year of Faith.*

ticularly strong centrifugal and disruptive forces at work today. A distinctive aspect of ecclesial communion is allegiance of mind and heart to the Magisterium of the Bishops, an allegiance which must be lived honestly and clearly testified to before the People of God by all consecrated persons, especially those involved in theological research, teaching, publishing, catechesis and the use of the means of social communication. Because consecrated persons have a special place in the Church, their attitude in this regard is of immense importance for the whole People of God" (n. 46).

The Holy See acknowledges with gratitude the great contribution of women Religious to the Church in the United States as seen particularly in the many schools, hospitals, and institutions of support for the poor which have been founded and staffed by Religious over the years. Pope John Paul II expressed this gratitude well in his meeting with Religious from the United States in San Francisco on September 17, 1987, when he said: *I rejoice because of your deep love of the Church and your generous service to God's people...The extensive Catholic educational and health care systems, the highly developed network of social services in the Church - none of this would exist today, were it not for your highly motivated dedication and the dedication of those who have gone before you. The spiritual vigor of so many Catholic people testifies to the efforts of generations of religious in this land. The history of the Church in this country is in large measure your history at the service of God's people.* The renewal of the Leadership Conference of Women Religious which is the goal of this doctrinal Assessment is in support of this essential charism of Religious which has been so obvious in the life and growth of the Catholic Church in the United States.

While recognizing that this doctrinal Assessment concerns a particular conference of major superiors and therefore does not intend to offer judgment on the faith and life of Women Religious in the member Congregations which belong to that conference, nevertheless the Assessment reveals serious doctrinal problems which affect many in Consecrated Life. On the doctrinal level, this crisis is characterized by a diminution of the fundamental Christological center and focus of religious consecration which leads, in turn, to a loss of a "constant and lively sense of the Church" among some Religious. The current doctrinal Assessment arises out of a sincere concern for the life of faith in some Institutes of Consecrated Life and Societies of Apostolic Life. It arises as well from a conviction that the work of any conference of major superiors of women Religious can and should be a fruitful means of addressing the contemporary situation and supporting religious life in its most "radical" sense—that is, in the <u>faith</u> in which it is rooted. According to Canon Law, conferences of major superiors are an expression of the collaboration between the Holy See, Superiors General, and the local Conferences of Bishops in support of consecrated life. The overarching concern of the doctrinal Assessment is, therefore, to assist the Leadership Conference of Women Religious in the United States in implementing an ecclesiology of communion founded on faith in Jesus Christ and the Church as the essential foundation for its important service to religious Communities and to all those in consecrated life.

II. The Doctrinal Assessment

The decision of the Congregation for the Doctrine of the Faith (CDF) to undertake a doctrinal Assessment of the Leadership Conference of Women Religious (LCWR) was communicated to the LCWR Presidency during their meeting with Cardinal William Levada in Rome on April 8, 2008. At that meeting, three major areas of concern were given as motivating the CDF's decision to initiate the Assessment:

- **Addresses at the LCWR Assemblies.** Addresses given during LCWR annual Assemblies manifest problematic statements and serious theological, even doctrinal errors. The Cardinal offered as an example specific passages of Sr. Laurie Brink's address about some Religious "moving beyond the Church" or even beyond Jesus. This is a challenge not only to core Catholic beliefs; such a rejection of faith is also a serious source of scandal and is incompatible with religious life. Such unacceptable positions routinely go unchallenged by the LCWR, which should provide resources for member Congregations to foster an ecclesial vision of religious life, thus helping to correct an erroneous vision of the Catholic faith as an important exercise of charity. Some might see in Sr. Brink's analysis a phenomenological snapshot of religious life today. But Pastors of the Church should also see in it a cry for help.

- **Policies of Corporate Dissent.** The Cardinal spoke of this issue in reference to letters the CDF received from "Leadership Teams" of various Congregations, among them LCWR Officers, protesting the Holy See's actions regarding the question of women's ordination and of a correct pastoral approach to ministry to homosexual persons, e.g. letters about New Ways Ministry's conferences. The terms of the letters suggest that these sisters collectively take a position not in agreement with the Church's teaching on human sexuality. It is a serious matter when these Leadership Teams are not providing effective leadership and example to their communities, but place themselves outside the Church's teaching.

o **Radical Feminism.** The Cardinal noted a prevalence of certain radical feminist themes incompatible with the Catholic faith in some of the programs and presentations sponsored by the LCWR, including theological interpretations that risk distorting faith in Jesus and his loving Father who sent his Son for the salvation of the world. Moreover, some commentaries on "patriarchy" distort the way in which Jesus has structured sacramental life in the Church; others even undermine the revealed doctrines of the Holy Trinity, the divinity of Christ, and the inspiration of Sacred Scripture.

Subsequently, in a letter dated February 18, 2009, the CDF confirmed its decision to undertake a doctrinal Assessment of the LCWR and named Most Rev. Leonard Blair, Bishop of Toledo, as the CDF's Delegate for the Assessment. This decision was further discussed with the LCWR Presidency during their visit to the CDF on April 22, 2009. During that meeting, Cardinal Levada confirmed that the doctrinal Assessment comes as a result of several years of examination of the doctrinal content of statements from the LCWR and of their annual conferences. The Assessment's primary concern is the doctrine of the faith that has been revealed by God in Jesus Christ, presented in written form in the divinely inspired Scriptures, and handed on in the Apostolic Tradition under the guidance of the Church's Magisterium. It is this Apostolic teaching, so richly and fully taught by the Second Vatican Council, that should underlie the work of a conference of major superiors of Religious which, by its nature, has a canonical relationship to the Holy See and many of whose members are of Pontifical right.

Most Rev. Leonard Blair communicated a set of doctrinal *Observations* to the LCWR in a letter dated May 11, 2009, and subsequently met with the Presidency on May 27, 2009. The LCWR Presidency responded to the *Observations* in a letter dated October 20, 2009. Based on this response, and on subsequent correspondence between the Presidency of the LCWR and the Delegate, Bishop Blair submitted his findings to the CDF on December 22, 2009.

On June 25, 2010, Bishop Blair presented further documentation on the content of the LCWR's *Mentoring Leadership Manual* and also on the organizations associated with the LCWR, namely *Network* and *The Resource Center for Religious Institutes*. The documentation reveals that, while there has been a great deal of work on the part of LCWR promoting issues of social justice in harmony with the Church's social doctrine, it is silent on the right to life from conception to natural death, a question that is part of the lively public debate about abortion and euthanasia in the United States. Further, issues of crucial importance to the life of Church and society, such as the Church's Biblical view of family life and human sexuality, are not part of the LCWR agenda in a way that promotes Church teaching. Moreover, occasional public statements by the LCWR that disagree with or challenge positions taken by the Bishops, who are the Church's authentic teachers of faith and morals, are not compatible with its purpose.

All of the documentation from the doctrinal Assessment including the LCWR responses was presented to the Ordinary Session of the Cardinal and Bishop Members of the CDF on January 12, 2011. The decision of that Ordinary Session was:

1) The current doctrinal and pastoral situation of the LCWR is grave and a matter of serious concern, also given the influence the LCWR exercises on religious Congregations in other parts of the world;

2) After the currently-ongoing Visitation of religious communities of women in the United States is brought to a conclusion, the Holy See should intervene with the prudent steps necessary to effect a reform of the LCWR;

3) The Congregation for the Doctrine of the Faith will examine the various forms of canonical intervention available for the resolution of the problematic aspects present in the LCWR.

The Holy Father, Pope Benedict XVI, in an Audience granted to the Prefect of the Congregation for the Doctrine of the Faith, Cardinal William Joseph Levada, on January 14, 2011, approved the decisions of the Ordinary Session of the Congregation, and ordered their implementation. This action by the Holy Father should be understood in virtue of the mandate given by the Lord to Simon Peter as the rock on which He founded his Church (cf. Luke 22:32): "I have prayed for you, Peter, that your faith may not fail; and when you have turned to me, you must strengthen the faith of your brothers and sisters." This Scripture passage has long been applied to the role of the Successors of Peter as Head of the Apostolic College of Bishops; it also applies to the role of the Pope as Chief Shepherd and Pastor of the Universal Church. Not least among the flock to whom the Pope's pastoral concern is directed are women Religious of apostolic life, who through the past several centuries have been so instrumental in building up the faith and life of the Holy Church of God, and witnessing to God's love for humanity in so many charitable and apostolic works.

Since the Final Report of the Apostolic Visitation of women Religious in the United States has now been submitted to the Holy See (in December, 2011), the CDF turns to the implementation of the above-mentioned decisions approved by the Holy Father as an extension of his pastoral outreach to the Church in the

United States. For the purpose of this implementation, and in consultation with the Congregation for Institutes of Consecrated Life and Societies of Apostolic Life (CICLSAL) and the Congregation for Bishops, the Congregation for the Doctrine of the Faith has decided to execute the mandate to assist in the necessary reform of the Leadership Conference of Women Religious through the appointment of a Archbishop Delegate, who will – with the assistance of a group of advisors (bishops, priests, and women Religious) – proceed to work with the leadership of the LCWR to achieve the goals necessary to address the problems outlined in this statement. The mandate given to the Delegate provides the structure and flexibility for the delicate work of such implementation.

The moment for such a common effort seems all the more opportune in view of an implementation of the recommendations of the recent Apostolic Visitation of women Religious in the United States, and in view of this year's 50th anniversary of the beginning of the Second Vatican Council, whose theological vision and practical recommendations for Consecrated Life can serve as a providential template for review and renewal of religious life in the United States, and of the mandate of Church law for the work of this conference of major superiors to which the large majority of congregations of women Religious in the United States belong.

III. Implementation: Conclusions of Doctrinal Assessment and Mandate

1) Principal Findings of the Doctrinal Assessment

LCWR General Assemblies, Addresses, and Occasional Papers

One of the principal means by which the LCWR promotes its particular vision of religious life is through the annual Assemblies it sponsors. During the Assessment process, Bishop Blair, in his letter of May 11, 2009, presented the LCWR Presidency with a study and doctrinal evaluation of keynote addresses, presidential addresses, and Leadership Award addresses over a 10 year period. This study found that the talks, while not scholarly theological discourses *per se*, do have significant doctrinal and moral content and implications which often contradict or ignore magisterial teaching.

In its response, the Presidency of the LCWR maintained that it does not knowingly invite speakers who take a stand against a teaching of the Church "when it has been declared as authoritative teaching." Further, the Presidency maintains that the assertions made by speakers are their own and do not imply intent on the part of the LCWR. Given the facts examined, however, this response is inadequate. The Second Vatican Council clearly indicates that an authentic teaching of the Church calls for the religious submission of intellect and will, and is not limited to defined dogmas or *ex cathedra* statements (cf. *Lumen gentium*, 25). For example, the LCWR publicly expressed in 1977 its refusal to assent to the teaching of *Inter insigniores* on the reservation of priestly ordination to men. This public refusal has never been corrected. Beyond this, the CDF understands that speakers at conferences or general assemblies do not submit their texts for prior review by the LCWR Presidency. But, as the Assessment demonstrated, the sum of those talks over the years is a matter of serious concern.

Several of the addresses at LCWR conferences present a vision or description of religious life that does not conform to the faith and practice of the Church. Since the LCWR leadership has offered no clarification about such statements, some might infer that such positions are endorsed by them. As an entity approved by the Holy See for the coordination and support of religious Communities in the United States, LCWR also has a positive responsibility for the promotion of the faith and for providing its member Communities and the wider Catholic public with clear and persuasive positions in support of the Church's vision of religious life.

Some speakers claim that dissent from the doctrine of the Church is justified as an exercise of the prophetic office. But this is based upon a mistaken understanding of the dynamic of prophecy in the Church: it justifies dissent by positing the possibility of divergence between the Church's magisterium and a "legitimate" theological intuition of some of the faithful. "Prophecy," as a methodological principle, is here directed *at* the Magisterium and the Church's pastors, whereas true prophecy is a grace which accompanies the exercise of the responsibilities of the Christian life and ministries within the Church, regulated and verified by the Church's faith and teaching office. Some of the addresses at LCWR-sponsored events perpetuate a distorted ecclesiological vision, and have scant regard for the role of the Magisterium as the guarantor of the authentic interpretation of the Church's faith.

The analysis of the General Assemblies, Presidential Addresses, and *Occasional Papers* reveals, therefore, a two-fold problem. The first consists in positive error (i.e. doctrinally problematic statements or formal refutation of Church teaching found in talks given at LCWR-sponsored conferences or General Assemblies). The second level of the problem concerns the silence and inaction of the LCWR in the face of such error, given its responsibility to support a vision of religious life in harmony with that of the Church and to promote a solid doctrinal basis for religious life. With this Assessment, the CDF intends to assist the LCWR in placing its activity into a wider context of religious life in the universal Church in order to foster a vision of consecrated life consistent with the Church's teaching. In this wider context, the CDF notes the absence of initiatives by the LCWR aimed at promoting the reception of the Church's teaching, especially on difficult issues such as Pope John Paul II's Apostolic Letter *Ordinatio sacerdotalis* and Church teaching about homosexuality.

The Role of the LCWR in the Doctrinal Formation of Religious Superiors and Formators

The program for new Superiors and Formators of member Communities and other resources provided to these Communities is an area in which the LCWR exercises an influence. The doctrinal Assessment found that many of the materials prepared by the LCWR for these purposes (*Occasional Papers, Systems Thinking Handbook*) do not have a sufficient doctrinal foundation. These materials recommend strategies for dialogue, for example when sisters disagree about basic matters of Catholic faith or moral practice, but it is not clear whether this dialogue is directed towards reception of Church teaching. As a case in point, the *Systems Thinking Handbook* presents a situation in which sisters differ over whether the Eucharist should be at the center of a special community celebration since the celebration of Mass requires an ordained priest, something which some sisters find "objectionable." According to the *Systems Thinking Handbook* this difficulty is rooted in differences at the level of belief, but also in different cognitive models (the "Western mind" as opposed to an "Organic mental model"). These models, rather than the teaching of the Church, are offered as tools for the resolution of the controversy of whether or not to celebrate Mass. Thus the *Systems Thinking Handbook* presents a neutral model of Congregational leadership that does not give due attention to the responsibility which Superiors are called to exercise, namely, leading sisters into a greater appreciation or integration of the truth of the Catholic faith.

The Final Report of the Apostolic Visitation of Religious Communities of Women in the United States (July, 2011) found that the formation programs among several communities that belong to the LCWR did not have significant doctrinal content but rather were oriented toward professional formation regarding particular issues of ministerial concern to the Institute. Other programs reportedly stressed their own charism and history, and/or the Church's social teaching or social justice in general, with little attention to basic Catholic doctrine, such as that contained in the authoritative text of the *Catechism of the Catholic Church.*

While these formation programs were not directly the object of this doctrinal Assessment, it may nevertheless be concluded that confusion about the Church's authentic doctrine of the faith is reinforced, rather than corrected, by the lack of doctrinal content in the resources provided by the LCWR for Superiors and Formators. The doctrinal confusion which has undermined solid catechesis over the years demonstrates the need for sound doctrinal formation—both initial and ongoing—for women Religious and novices just as it does for priests and seminarians, and for laity in ministry and apostolic life. In this way, we can hope that the secularized contemporary culture, with its negative impact on the very identity of Religious as Christians and members of the Church, on their religious practice and common life, and on their authentic Christian spirituality, moral life, and liturgical practice, can be more readily overcome.

2) The Mandate for Implementation of the Doctrinal Assessment

In the universal law of the Church (Code of Canon Law [C.I.C.] for the Latin Church), Canons 708 and 709 address the establishment and work of conferences of major superiors:

Can. 708: Major superiors can be associated usefully in conferences or councils so that by common efforts they work to achieve more fully the purpose of the individual institutes, always without prejudice to their autonomy, character, and proper spirit, or to transact common affairs, or to establish appropriate coordination and cooperation with the conferences of bishops and also with individual bishops.

Can. 709: Conferences of major superiors are to have their own statutes approved by the Holy See, by which alone they can be erected even as a juridic person and under whose supreme direction they remain.

In the light of these canons, and in view of the findings of the doctrinal Assessment, it is clear that greater emphasis needs to be placed both on the relationship of the LCWR with the Conference of Bishops, and on the need to provide a sound doctrinal foundation in the faith of the Church as they "work to achieve more fully the purpose of the individual institutes."

Therefore in order to implement a process of review and conformity to the teachings and discipline of the Church, the Holy See, through the Congregation for the Doctrine of the Faith, will appoint an Archbishop Delegate, assisted by two Bishops, for review, guidance and approval, where necessary, of the work of the LCWR. The Delegate will report to the CDF, which will inform and consult with the Congregation for Institutes of Consecrated Life and Societies of Apostolic Life and the Congregation for Bishops.

The mandate of the Delegate is to include the following:

1) To revise LCWR Statutes to ensure greater clarity about the scope of the mission and responsibilities of this conference of major superiors. The revised Statutes will be submitted to the Holy See for approval by the CICLSAL.

2) To review LCWR plans and programs, including General Assemblies and publications, to ensure that the scope of the LCWR's mission is fulfilled in accord with Church teachings and discipline. In particular:

–*Systems Thinking Handbook* will be withdrawn from circulation pending revision

–LCWR programs for (future) Superiors and Formators will be reformed

–Speakers/presenters at major programs will be subject to approval by Delegate

3) To create new LCWR programs for member Congregations for the development of initial and ongoing formation material that provides a deepened understanding of the Church's doctrine of the faith.

4) To review and offer guidance in the application of liturgical norms and texts. For example:

–The Eucharist and the Liturgy of the Hours will have a place of priority in LCWR events and programs.

5) To review LCWR links with affiliated organizations, e.g. Network and Resource Center for Religious Life.

The mandate of the Delegate will be for a period of up to five years, as deemed necessary. In order to ensure the necessary liaison with the USCCB (in view of Can. 708), the Conference of Bishops will be asked to establish a formal link (e.g. a committee structure) with the Delegate and Assistant Delegate Bishops. In order to facilitate the achievement of these goals, the Delegate is authorized to form an Advisory Team (clergy, women Religious, and experts) to assist in the work of implementation.

It will be the task of the Archbishop Delegate to work collaboratively with the officers of the LCWR to achieve the goals outlined in this document, and to report on the progress of this work to the Holy See. Such reports will be reviewed with the Delegate at regular interdicasterial meetings of the CDF and the CICLSAL. In this way, the Holy See hopes to offer an important contribution to the future of religious life in the Church in the United States.

****

Canon 930 §2

Use of Older English Translation of Roman Missal by Elderly Priests Retired from Active Ministry

The diocesan bishop of a United States diocese was concerned about some elderly retired priests, living at the Priests' Retirement Center, who had expressed anxiety about whether they would be able to adapt to the new Roman Missal with their diminished vision and failing mental capacity. On their behalf, the bishop wrote to the Congregation for Divine Worship and the Discipline of the Sacraments. Below is the response from the Congregation.

CONGREGATION FOR DIVINE WORSHIP AND
DISCIPLINE OF THE SACRAMENTS
Prot. N.______

Your Excellency,

This Congregation for Divine Worship and Discipline of the Sacraments writes in response to your letter of ______, regarding the possible use of the older English translation of the Roman Missal by certain elderly priests who are retired from active ministry.

The Congregation is willing for those with genuine need to be thus accommodated, so long as the celebration is in a "private" setting. As moderator of the Sacred Liturgy for the Diocese of ______, Your Excellency will need to exercise care to ensure the proper use of any such exceptions to standard practice. Of course, this limited group of retired priests is to be encouraged insofar as possible to learn and make use of the new translation.

With best wishes and kind regards, I am

Sincerely yours in Christ,

(signed)
+J. Augustine DiNoia, O.P.
Archbishop Secretary

Canon 1041, 4°

Dispensation from Irregularity for Reception of Orders for Assistance in Procurement of an Abortion

A diocesan bishop requested a dispensation from the irregularity for the reception of Orders from the Apostolic Penitentiary for a candidate for the permanent diaconate who, earlier in his life, had assisted in the procurement of an abortion of his child. The response of the Apostolic Penitentiary follows.

APOSTOLIC PENITENTIARY
Prot. N. ______

Excellency,

In response to the request that your candidate for the permanent diaconate be dispensed from the irregularity for the reception of Orders (canon 1041, 4°), incurred because of positive assistance in the procurement of the abortion of his child, this Apostolic Penitentiary hastens to answer as follows.

Considering the circumstances of the case: the lapse of 14 years from the crime, the anguish and remorse the candidate subsequently went through and which led him to deeper conversion and growth in the Catholic faith, the absence of any danger of scandal and above all your request made on his behalf, which indicates that you judge him suitable for Orders, this Apostolic Penitentiary, judging the candidate worthy to be dispensed from the irregularity, "*ex Apostolica Auctoritate*" grants to you, Excellency, the faculty to dispense the petitioner from the irregularity incurred. This is to be done in the internal forum, sacramental or non-sacramental, whichever you deem more opportune.

This Rescript belongs exclusively to the forum of conscience, and therefore, if knowledge of it did not come from the Sacrament of Reconciliation, then the Rescript, after its execution, should be signed and dated, and kept in the secret archives of the Diocese; otherwise, it should be destroyed.

Excellency, in matters dealt with by this Dicastery, the identity of the person involved should, if at all possible, be kept secret. Therefore the candidate's name will be deleted from the documents which were sent here. Also, all that is needed is an articulate presentation of the case by yourself, and your opinion regarding the suitableness of the candidate for Orders. The candidate's *curriculum vitae* and presentation of the case is helpful. If the one requesting a dispensation is a candidate for the priesthood, the policy of the Penitentiary is not to grant the dispensation until the person has been approved for Orders, namely 6 months before ordination. There is no need to send three copies of the request and documents.

With best wishes for a blessed and happy Easter, we are, Your Excellency,

Sincerely yours in the Lord Jesus,

(signed)
Manuel Cardinal Monteiro de Castro
Major Penitentiary

(Signed)
+Gianfranco Girotti, O.F.M., Conv.
Regent

CANON 1127 §2

DISPENSATION FROM CANONICAL FORM FOR MARRIAGE OF A CATHOLIC AND A LUTHERAN WHO HAD BEEN BAPTIZED A CATHOLIC IN INFANCY

A diocesan bishop requested from the Congregation for Divine Worship and Discipline of the Sacraments a dispensation from canonical form for a Catholic and a Lutheran baptized a Catholic to be married in a Lutheran church. The Congregation's response follows.

CONGREGATION FOR DIVINE WORSHIP AND
DISCIPLINE OF THE SACRAMENTS
Prot. N. ______

Your Eminence,

In your letter of April 27, 2012, you request dispensation from the canonical form of marriage (cf. can. 1127, §2), so that Mary ______, a Catholic of the (Arch)diocese of ______ and John ______, a Lutheran who had been baptized a Catholic in his infancy, might be married at ______ Lutheran Church in ______, on ______, 2012.

In light of the urgency of this request, this Congregation for Divine Worship and Discipline of the Sacraments does hereby grant, by means of this same letter, the requested dispensation from the requirement of can. 1127, §2, on behalf of Mary ______ and John ______.

It is be borne in mind, however, since the city of ______, where the marriage it to take place, lies in the Diocese of ______, it will be necessary – if it has not already been done – in accord with the requirement of the aforementioned canon, to consult with the Ordinary of that Diocese about this request.

Sincerely yours in Christ,

(signed)
+J. Augustine DiNoia, OP
Archbishop Secretary

CANON 1292 §1

COMPLEMENTARY LEGISLATION REVISING LIMITS ON ALIENATION

Following two biennial extensions of the 2002 approved complementary legislation for the implementation of canon 1292 §1 for the dioceses of the United States, the Congregation for Bishops granted a definitive recognitio *for the defined limits in March 2010. A subsequent decree by the same Congregation was issued May 10, 2011 granting a definitive* recognitio *to norm 3 of the complementary legislation. The Decree of Promulgation by then-Archbishop Timothy Dolan, President of the United States Conference of Catholic Bishops, follows.*

UNITED STATES CONFERENCE OF CATHOLIC BISHOPS

DECREE OF PROMULGATION

On November 13, 2002, the Latin Church members of the United States Conference of Catholic Bishops approved complementary legislation for the implementation of canon 1292, §1 of the *Code of Canon Law* for the dioceses of the United States. The action was granted recognition by the Congregation for Bishops in accord with article 82 of the Apostolic Constitution *Pastor bonus*, issued by a Decree (Prot. N. 296/84) of the Congregation for Bishops, dated June 3, 2003, and signed by His Eminence Giovanni Battista Cardinal Re, Prefect, and His Excellency Most Reverend Franciscus Monterisi, Secretary. On March 31, 2004, a subsequent Decree with the same Protocol Number was issued granting recognition to the norms *ad biennium*. Through subsequent Decrees, dated January 31, 2006 and March 31, 2008, again with the same aforementioned Protocol Number, the same Congregation decreed the extension of its previously granted *recognitio* for two additional two-year periods. By means of a Decree, dated March 31, 2010 (Prot. N. 778/2005), signed by His Eminence Giovanni Battista Cardinal Re, Prefect, and His Excellency Most Reverend Manuel Monteiro de Castro, Secretary, the Congregation for Bishops granted definitive recognition to the following defined sums. A subsequent Decree, dated May 10, 2011, with the same aforementioned Protocol Number, signed by His Excellency Most Reverend Manuel Monteiro de Castro, Secretary, and His Excellency Most Reverend Giovanni Maria Rossi, Subsecretary, granted definitive recognition to the sums defined in norm 3 of the complementary legislation.

Wherefore, and in accord with the prescripts of canon 1292, §1 the United States Conference of Catholic Bishops decrees that:

1. The maximum limit for alienation and any transaction which, according to the norm of law, can worsen the patrimonial condition is $7,500,000 for Dioceses with Catholic populations of half a million persons or more. For other Dioceses the maximum limit is $3,500,000 (cf. can. 1295).

2. The minimum limit for alienation and any transaction which, according to the norm of law, can worsen the patrimonial condition is $750,000 for Dioceses with Catholic populations of half a million persons or more. For other Dioceses the minimum is $250,000.

3. For the alienation of property of other public juridic persons subject to the Diocesan Bishop, the maximum limit is $3,500,000 and the minimum limit is $25,000 or 10% of the prior year's ordinary annual income, whichever is higher.

As President of the United States Conference of Catholic Bishops, I hereby decree that these norms are effective immediately for all dioceses of the United States Conference of Catholic Bishops.

Given at the offices of the United States Conference of Catholic Bishops, in the city of Washington, the District of Columbia, on the 1st of December, in the year of Our Lord 2011.

(signed)
Most Reverend Timothy M. Dolan
Archbishop of New York
President, USCCB

(signed)
Reverend Monsignor Ronny E. Jenkins
General Secretary, USCCB

Canons 1445 §3, 1475, and 1527

General Executory Decree
Regarding the Preservation of Judicial Acts

In response to questions from Episcopal Moderators and Judicial Vicars regarding the preservation of judicial acts, especially from cases of marriage nullity, the Apostolic Signatura, aware of the burden proper preservation creates for Tribunals, issued a general executory decree regulating this matter. An unofficial English tranlsation of the decree is presented, followed by the original Latin decree.

UNOFFICIAL ENGLISH TRANSLATION

SUPREME TRIBUNAL OF THE APOSTOLIC SIGNATURA

Often Episcopal Moderators and Judicial Vicars frequently transmit to this Supreme Tribunal observations and questions concerning the preservation of judicial acts, after trials have been completed. For the burden of keeping these acts weighs more heavily on Tribunals every day, especially on account of the more numerous cases of the nullity of marriage examined before Ecclesiastical Tribunals since the nineteen-seventies and also on account of the increased amount of judicial acts especially from the use of photocopying.

Up to now, this Apostolic Signatura has given responses in particular cases, allowing judicial acts to be destroyed after ten years from the conclusion of the process under two conditions, namely, that the original text of the decisions always be preserved and also that the remaining acts be kept by means of more recent technologies so that they can be reproduced in their entirety whenever there should be a need.

Nevertheless, to regulate this matter more aptly one does not want a single response for all Ecclesiastical Tribunals, since the economic or local circumstances affecting Tribunals are not of a single kind. On the other hand, it does not appear opportune to leave the matter to statutes or particular decisions, since abuses could insert themselves in a matter of such importance.

Having considered these matters,

THE SUPREME TRIBUNAL OF THE APOSTOLIC SIGNATURA

Holding as established the general principle according to which judicial acts, after the completion of a trial of the nullity of a marriage, must be preserved in the safest possible manner at least until the death of one or the other spouse, even using for this purpose more recent technological means, keeping , however, the definitive decisions in the original;

Attentive, however, to the increasingly heavier burdens which the proper preservation of judicial acts creates for Tribunals;

Observing moreover that it is the responsibility of the competent judge to curb an excessive quantity of acts, both by an attentive application of the canons (cf. especially can. 1527, §1; art. 157, §3, of the Instruction *Dignitas connubii*) and, whenever it is possible, by the more recent technological means, applied with due precautions;

Having considered the prescript of canon 489, §2, issued in a similar matter ;

Having confirmed the prescript of can. 1475, §1 (cf. art. 91, §1, of the above noted Instruction);

Having examined the prescripts of canons 1472, 1492, 1522, 1525, 1598, 1611, 1621, 1643, 1644, 1646, 1684 (cf. articles 88; 148; 151; 235, §1; 250; 271; 289, §1; 290 of the same Instruction);

With due regard for the laws of the Tribunals of the Apostolic See (can. 1402);

In virtue of articles 121 and 124, n. 1, of the Apostolic Constitution, *Pastor bonus* (cf. also can. 1445, §3), articles 32, 35 and 112 of the proper Law, by which this Supreme Tribunal is regulated, and also can. 31, §1;

After the matter had been carefully examined twice in Congresso before the undersigned Prefect;

Having heard the Pontifical Council for Legislative Texts according to the norm of art. 131, §5, of the General Regulation of the Roman Curia;

The text of this decree having been reviewed and recommended by the Cardinal and Bishop Members of the Supreme Tribunal of the Apostolic Signatura, in a plenary Session held on 3-4 February 2011 before the undersigned Prefect, and also having been presented to the Supreme Pontiff according to the norm of art. 131, §6, of the above noted Regulation, and having been approved by POPE BENEDICT XVI on 20 July 2011, has decreed:

If the preservation of judicial acts by any secure means whatsoever, even by the use of more recent technological means, constitutes a grave inconvenience, the Bishop Moderators of Ecclesiastical Tribunals have the competence, having duly pondered all of the circumstances, to issue norms concerning the destruction at fixed times of the judicial acts of cases of the nullity of marriage, under these conditions:

the cases in question have been concluded for at least twenty years;

concerning these individual cases, the definitive sentences, decrees of confirmation, decisions having the force of a definitive sentence and, if there by any, interlocutory pronouncements are to be preserved in the original text or in an authentic copy.

Given at Rome, from the Seat of the Supreme Tribunal of the Apostolic Signatura, on 13 August 2011.

(signed)
Raymond Leo Cardinal Burke
Prefect

(signed)
+Frans Daneels, O. Praem.
Secretary

Prot. N. 42027/08 VT

ACTA TRIBUNALIUM

Supremum Signaturae Apostolicae Tribunal

Decretum generale exsecutorium de actis iudicialibus conservandis

Saepe saepius Episcopi Moderatores et Vicarii iudiciales ad hoc Supremum Tribunal animadversions atque quaesita transmittunt de actis iudicialibus, post expleta iudicia, conservandis. Nam onus eadem asservandi in dies gravius Tribunalibus incumbit, praesertim ob numerosiores causas nullitatis matrimonii ab annis septuaginta praeteriti saeculi apud Tribunalia Ecclesiastica pertractatas necnon ob actorum iudicialium incrementum praesertim ex usu exemplarium luce impressa confectorum.

Usque adhuc haec Signatura Apostolica responsa dedit in casibus particularibus, acta iudicialia post decem annos a conclusione processus destrui posse concedens duabus sub condicionibus, id est, originales decisionum textus semper servandos esse atque cetera acta adhibitis mediis technicis recentioribus asservanda esse, ita ut integra reproduci possint quotiescumque opus sit.

Ad hanc materiam aptius moderandam, tamen, non una responsione pro omnibus Tribunalibus Ecclesiasticis opus est, cum adiuncta sive oeconomica sive loci, quibus Tribunalia afficiuntur, non unius generis sint. Nec, ceterum, opportunum apparet rem relinquere statutis vel decisionibus particularibus, cum abusus in re tanti momenti irrepere possint.

Quibus praehabitis,

SUPREMUM SIGNATURAE APOSTOLICAE TRIBUNAL

Pro comperto habito principio generali iuxta quod acta iudicialia, expleto nullitatis matrimonii iudicio, saltem usque ad mortem alterutrius coniugis conservanda sunt tutiore quo potest modo, etiam ad rem adhibitis mediis technicis recentioribus, decisionibus tamen definitivis sub originali servatis;

Perspectis autem oneribus in dies gravioribus, quae pro recta actorum iudicialium conservatione Tribunalibus incumbunt;

Animadverso ceterum quod iudicis competentis est nimiam actorum multitudinem refrenare sive ex sedula canonum applicatione (cf. praesertim can. 1527, §1; art. 157, §3 Instructionis *Dignitas connunii*) sive, quantum fieri potest, ex recentioribus mediis technicis, cum debitis cautelis applicandis;

Considerato canonis 489, §2 praescripto in re simili lato;

Firmo praescripto can. 1475, §1 (cf. art. 91, §1 praefatae Instructionis);

Visis praescriptis canonum 1472, 1492, 1522, 1525, 1598, 1611, 1621, 1643, 1644, 1646, 1684 (cf. artt. 88; 148; 151; 235, §1; 250; 271; 289, §1; 290 eiusdem Instructionis);

Salvis legibus Tribunalium Apostolicae Sedis (can. 1402);

Vi artt. 121 et 124, n. 1 Const. Apost. *Pastor bonus* (cf. etiam can. 1445, §3), artt. 32, 35, et 112 Legis propriae, qua hoc Supremum Tribunal regitur, atque can. 31, §1;

Re sedulo bis examini subiecta in Congressu coram infrascripto Praefecto habito;

Audito Pontificio Consilio de Legum Textibus ad normam art. 131, §5 Ordinationis generalis Romanae Curiae;

Huius decreti textu ab Em.mis et Exc.mis Patribus Supremi Signaturae Apostolicae Tribunalis, in plenario Coetu diebus 3-4 Februarii anni 2011 coram infrascripto Praefecto habito, recognito et probato, atque Summo Pontifici ad normam art. 131, §6 praefatae Ordinationis porrecto, eoque a BENEDICTO PP. XVI die 20 Iulii 2011 approbato,

DECREVIT

Si grave incommodum constituat actorum iudicialium conservatio, quocumque tuto modo peracta, etiam recentioribus mediis technicis abhibitis, Episcopis Moderatoribus Tribunalium Ecclesiasticorum competere ut, omnibus adiunctis aeque ponderatis, normas edant de actis iudicialibus causarum nullitatis matrimonii, statutis temporibus, destruendis, his sub condicionibus:

- causas *de quibus* saltem a viginti annis conclusae sint;
- de iisdem singulis causis semper serventur, sub textu originali vel exemplari authentico, sententiae definitivae, decreta confirmatoria, decisiones vim sententiae definitivae habentes et, si quae sint, pronuntiationes interlocutoriae.

Datum Romae, e Sede Supremi Signaturae Apostolicae Tribunalis, die 13 Augusti 2011.

(signed)
Raimundus Leo S.R.E. Card. Burke
Praefectus

(signed)
+Franciscus Daneels, O. Praem.
Secretarius

Prot. N. 42027/08 VT

Canon 1445 §3, 2°

Decree of the Supreme Tribunal on Judicial Cases of the Syriac Eparchy in Canada and the United States

At the request of the Eparchial bishop of Our Lady of Deliverance of the Syriacs that the adjudication of judicial cases of the Christian faithful of the eparchy living in the United States be committed to the tribunal of the Eparchy of Saint Maron of Brooklyn, the Apostolic Signatura issued a decree, responding to the request. An unofficial English translation of the decree is presented, followed by the original Latin decree.

UNOFFICIAL ENGLISH TRANSLATION

SUPREME TRIBUNAL OF THE APOSTOLIC SIGNATURA

Prot. No. 1126/1/12 SAT

With the apostolic constitution *Principis Apostolorum,* the Roman Pontiff John Paul II erected in 1995 the Eparchy for the Syriac Christian faithful of the Antiochene Church in the United States of America also with jurisdiction for those residing in Canada named under the title of *Our Lady of Deliverance of the Syriacs*.

With the decree of 20 March 1997, the Apostolic Signatura committed the judicial cases of this eparchy to the eparchial tribunal of the Eparchy of Saint-Sauveur de Montréal for the first instance until provided otherwise.

With the letter of 26 January 2012, the Most Reverend Eparchial bishop of Our Lady of Deliverance petitioned that, without prejudice to the decree of 20 March 1997 for the Canadian Christian faithful of the eparchy, that judicial cases of the Christian faithful in the United States of America of the eparchy be committed for adjudication to the tribunal of the Eparchy of Saint Maron of Brooklyn for the Maronites.

In consideration of the foregoing, the Supreme Tribunal of the Apostolic Signatura, having carefully examined the matter and considered the reasons;

Given that the Most Reverend Moderators of the tribunal of Saint Maron of

Brooklyn for the Maronites and of the tribunal of Newton for the Melkite Greek Catholics gave their consent;

Having heard the Reverend Promotor of Justice;

In virtue of art. 124, n. 3 of the Apostolic Constitution *Pastor bonus* (cf. also CIC c. 1445 §3, n. 2) and art. 35, n. 3 of the proper law by which this Supreme Tribunal is governed [Pope Benedict XVI, mp *Antiqua Ordinatione*, 21 June 2008-ed.],

decreed:

> That requested extension be granted so that, without prejudice to the decree of 20 March 1997 for the Christian faithful in the jurisdiction of Canada, judicial causes for the Christian faithful in the Eparchy of Our Lady of Deliverance for the Syriacs residing in the United States of America be committed to the tribunal of Saint Maron of Brooklyn for the Maronites in the first instance to be examined and resolved.

Given in Rome at the offices of the Supreme Tribunal of the Apostolic Signatura on 28 February 2012.

(signed)
Raymond Leo Cardinal Burke
Prefect

(signed)
+Frans Daneels, O. Praem.
Secretary

SUPREMUM SIGNATURAE APOSTOLICAE TRIBUNAL

Prot. N. 1126/1/12 SAT

Constitutione Apostolica *Principis Apostolorum* Summus Pontifex Ioannes Paulus II, f.r., Eparchiam pro christifidelibus Ecclesiae Antiochenae Syrorum in Civitatibus Foederatis Americae Septentrionalis necnon dicione Canadensi digentibus titulo *Dominae Nostrae Liberationis Novarcensis Syrorum* nuncupatam anno 1995 erexit.

Cuius Eparchiae causas iudiciarias, decreto die 20 martii 1997, haec Signatura Apostolica Tribunali Eparchiali Sanctissimi Salvatoris Marianopolitano

Graecorum Melkitarum iudicandas in primo gradu, donec aliter provideretur, commisit.

Litteris die 26 ianuarii 2012 datis, Exc.mus Episcopus Eparchialis Dominae Nostrae Liberationis Novarcensis Syrorum petiit ut, firmo manente decreto diei 20 martii 1997 pro christifidelibus in dicione Canadensi Eparchiae, causae iudiciariae christifidelium in Americae Septentrionalis Civitatibus Foederatis eiusdem Eparchiae Foro Sancti Maronis Bruklyniensis Maronitarum iudicandas committerentur.

Quibus praehabitis,

SUPREMUM SIGNATURAE APOSTOLICAE TRIBUNAL

Re sedulo examini subiecta atque rationibus adductis apte consideratis;

Attento quod Exc.mi Moderatores sive Tribunalis Sancti Maronis Bruklyniensis Maronitarum sive Tribunalis Neotoniensis Graecorum Melkitarum suum dederunt consensum;

Audito Rev.mo Promotore Iustitiae;

Vi art. 124, n. 3, Const. Ap. *Pastor bonus* (cf. etiam can. 1445, §3, n. 2) et art. 35, n. 3 *Legis propriae,* qua H.S.T. regitur,

decrevit:

Petitam prorogationem concedi adeo ut, firmo manente decreto diei 20 martii 1997 pro christifidelibus in dicione Canadensi, causae iudiciariae christifidelium Eparchiae Dominae Nostrae Liberationis Novarcensis Syrorum in Civitatibus Foederatis Americae Septentrionalis digentibus Tribunali Sancti Maronis Bruklyniensis Maronitarum in primo gradu pertractandae ac definiendae committantur.

Datum Romae, e Sede Supremi Signaturae Apostolicae Tribunalis, die 28 februarii 2012.

(signed)
Raimundus Leo Card. Burke
Praefectus

(signed)
+Franciscus Daneels, O. Praem.
Secretarius

Anglicanorum Coetibus, Art. 1 §§1-2

Decree of Erection of the Personal Ordinariate

In accord with the provisions of the apostolic consitution Anglicanorum coetibus *of Pope Benedict XVI (November 4, 2009) and after having consulted the United States Conference of Catholic Bishops, the Congregation for the Doctrine of the Faith issued a decree erecting a personal ordinariate within the territory of the Episcopal Conference of the United States for those groups of Anglican clergy and faithful who have expressed their desire to enter into full visible communion with the Catholic Church.*

CONGREGATION FOR THE DOCTRINE OF THE FAITH

Decree of Erection of the Personal Ordinariate
of the Chair of Saint Peter

The supreme law of the Church is the salvation of souls. As such, throughout its history, the Church has always found the pastoral and juridical means to care for the good of the faithful.

With the Apostolic Constitution *Anglicanorum coetibus*, promulgated on 4 November 2009, the Holy Father, Pope Benedict XVI, provided for the establishment of Personal Ordinariates through which Anglican faithful may enter, even in a corporate manner, into full communion with the Catholic Church.[1] On that same date, the Congregation for the Doctrine of the Faith published *Complementary Norms* relating to such Ordinariates.[2]

In conformity with what is established in Art. I §1 and §2 of the Apostolic Constitution *Anglicanorum coetibus*, having received requests from a considerable number of Anglican faithful, and having consulted with the United States Conference of Catholic Bishops, the Congregation for the Doctrine of the Faith

ERECTS

the Personal Ordinariate of the Chair of Saint Peter within the territory of the Episcopal Conference of the United States.

1 Cf. *AAS* 101 (2009), 985-990.

2 Cf. *L'Osservatore Romano* (9-10 November 2009), p. 7; Weekly Edition in English (11 November 2009), p. 4.

1. The Personal Ordinariate of the Chair of Saint Peter *ipso iure* possesses juridic personality and is juridically equivalent to a diocese.[3] It includes those faithful, of every category and state of life, who, originally having belonged to the Anglican Communion, are now in full communion with the Catholic Church, or who have received the sacraments of initiation within the jurisdiction of the Ordinariate itself,[4] or who are received into it because they are part of a family belonging to the Ordinariate.[5]

2. The faithful of the Personal Ordinariate of the Chair of Saint Peter are entrusted to the pastoral care of the Personal Ordinary who, once named by the Roman Pontiff,[6] possesses all the faculties, and is held to all the obligations, specified in the Apostolic Constitution *Anglicanorum* and the *Complementary Norms*[7] as well as in those matters determined subsequently by the Congregation for the Doctrine of the Faith, on request both of the Ordinary, having heard the Governing Council of the Ordinariate, and of the United States Conference of Catholic Bishops.

3. The Anglican faithful who wish to be received into full communion with the Catholic Church through the Ordinariate must manifest this desire in writing.[8] There is to be a programme of catechetical formation for these faithful, lasting for a congruent time, and with content established by the Ordinary in agreement with the Congregation for the Doctrine of the Faith so that the faithful are able to adhere fully to the doctrinal content of the *Catechism of the Catholic Church*,[9] and therefore, make the profession of faith.

4. For candidates for ordination, who previously were ministers in the Anglican Communion, there is to be a specific programme of theological formation, as well as spiritual and pastoral preparation, prior to ordination in the Catholic Church, according to what will be established by the Ordinary in agreement with the Congregation for the Doctrine of the Faith and in consultation with the United States Conference of Catholic Bishops.

5. For a cleric not incardinated in the Personal Ordinariate of the Chair of

3 Cf. can. 372 § 2 *CIC*; Apostolic Constitution *Anglicanorum coetibus*, Art. I § 3.

4 Cf. Apostolic Constitution *Anglicanorum coetibus*, Art. I § 4.

5 Cf. *Complementary Norms*, Art. 5 § 1.

6 Cf. Apostolic Constitution *Anglicanorum coetibus*, Art. IV, *Complementary Norms*, Art. 4 § 1.

7 Cf. Apostolic Constitution *Anglicanorum coetibus*, Art. VI § 4; *Complementary Norms*, Art. 5 § 2; Art. 9.

8 Cf. Apostolic Constitution *Anglicanorum coetibus*, Art. IX.

9 Cf. Apostolic Constitution *Anglicanorum coetibus*, Art. I § 5.

Saint Peter to assist at a marriage of the faithful belonging to the Ordinariate, he must receive the faculty from the Ordinary or the pastor of the personal parish to which the faithful belong.[10]

6. The Ordinary is a member by right of the United States Conference of Catholic Bishops, with deliberative vote in those cases in which this is required in law.[11]

7. A cleric, having come originally from the Anglican Communion, who has already been ordained in the Catholic Church and incardinated in a Diocese, is able to be incardinated in the Ordinariate in accord with the norm of can. 267 *CIC*.

8. Until the Personal Ordinariate of the Chair of Saint Peter may have established its own Tribunal, the judicial cases of its faithful are referred to the Tribunal of the Diocese in which one of the parties has a domicile, while taking into account, however, the different titles of competence established in cann. 1408-1414 and 1673 *CIC*.[12]

9. The faithful of the Personal Ordinariate of the Chair of Saint Peter who are, temporarily or permanently, outside the territory of the United States Conference of Catholic Bishops, while remaining members of the Ordinariate, are bound by universal law and those particular laws of the territory where they find themselves.[13]

10. If a member of the faithful moves permanently into a place where another Personal Ordinariate has been erected, he is able, on his own request, to be received into it. The new Ordinary is bound to inform the original Personal Ordinariate of the reception. If a member of the faithful wishes to leave the Ordinariate, he must make such a decision known to his own Ordinary. He automatically becomes a member of the Diocese where he resides. In this case, the Ordinary will ensure that the Diocesan Bishop is informed.

11. The Ordinary, keeping in mind the *Ratio fundamentalis institutionis sacerdotalis* and the *Programme of Priestly Formation* of the United States Conference of Catholic Bishops, is to prepare a *Programme of Priestly Formation* for the

10 Cf. cann. 1110-1111 *CIC*.

11 Cf. *Complementary Norms*, Art. 2 § 2.

12 Cf. Apostolic Constitution *Anglicanorum coetibus*, Art. XII.

13 Cf. can. 13 § 3 *CIC*.

seminarians of the Ordinariate which must be approved by the Apostolic See.[14]

12. The Ordinary will ensure that the Statutes of the Governing Council and the Pastoral Council, which are subject to his approval, are drawn up.[15]

13. The location of the principal Church of the Personal Ordinariate of the Chair of Saint Peter will be the Church of Our Lady of Walsingham in Houston, Texas. The Seat of the Ordinariate, where the register referred to in Art. 5 § 1 of the *Complementary Norms* will be kept, will be determined by the Ordinary in agreement with the Congregation for the Doctrine of the Faith and in consultation with the United States Conference of Catholic Bishops.

14. The Personal Ordinariate of the Chair of Saint Peter has as its patron the Blessed Virgin Mary under the title Our Lady of Walsingham.

Everything to the contrary notwithstanding.

Rome, from the Offices of the Congregation for the Doctrine of the Faith, 1 January 2012, the Solemnity of Mary, Mother of God.

(signed)
William Cardinal Levada
Prefect

+Luis F. Ladaria, S.I.
Secretary

14 Cf. *Complementary Norms*, Art. 10 § 3; see also Apostolic Constitution *Anglicanorum coetibus*, Art. VI § 2.

15 Cf. *Complementary Norms*, Art. 12 § 1; Art. 13 § 2.

Papal Address to the Roman Rota

Address of His Holiness Benedict XVI for the Inauguration of the Judicial Year Of the Tribunal of the Roman Rota

---

January 21, 2012

Dear Members of the Tribunal of the Roman Rota,

It is cause of joy for me to receive you today in this annual encounter, on the occasion of the inauguration of the judicial year. I extend my greetings to the College of Prelate Auditors, starting with the Dean, Bishop Stankiewicz, whom I thank for his words. Cordial greetings also to the Officials, the [Rotal] Advocates, and other collaborators, and to all those who are present. On this occasion, I renew my esteem for the delicate and precious ministry which you carry out in the Church and which requires an ever-renewed effort, account taken of the impact it has on the *salus animarum* of the People of God.

In the appointment of this year, I would like to begin with one of the most important ecclesial events which we will experience in a few months. I am referring to the *Year of Faith*, which, following in the footsteps of my Venerable Predecessor, the Servant of God Paul VI, I wanted to proclaim upon the 50th anniversary of the opening of the Second Ecumenical Vatican Council. That great Pontiff — as I wrote in the Apostolic Letter of Indiction — established for the first time that period of reflection "fully conscious of the grave difficulties of the time, especially with regard to the profession of the True Faith and its correct interpretation".[1]

Following a similar exigency, segueing to the subject matter which more directly concerns your service to the Church, today I would like to reflect upon a primary aspect of the judicial ministry, namely the interpretation of canonical law with respect to its application.[2] The connection to the theme just touched upon — the right interpretation of the Faith — certainly cannot be reduced to a mere semantic assonance, considering that Canon Law grounds its foundation and its very meaning in the Truths of the Faith, and that the *Lex Agendi* cannot

1 Motu Proprio *Porta Fidei*, 11 October 2011, 5: *L'Osservatore Romano*, 17-18 October 2011, p. 4.

2 Cf. can. 16, §3; can. 1498, §3 *CCEO*.

but mirror the *Lex Credendi*. The question of the interpretation of canonical law, moreover, constitutes a rather vast and complex subject, in front of which I will limit myself to making some observations.

All things considered, the hermeneutics of canonical laws is most closely tied to the very understanding of the law of the Church. Were one to tend to identify Canon Law with the system of the laws of the canons, the understanding of that which is juridical in the Church would essentially consist in the comprehending of that which the legal texts establish. At first glance, this approach would appear to hold Human Law entirely in value. However the impoverishment which this conception would bring about becomes manifest: with the practical oblivion of the Natural Law and of the Divine Positive Law, as well as the vital relationship of every Law with the communion and the mission of the Church, the work of the interpreter becomes deprived of vital contact with ecclesial reality.

In most recent times, some currents of thought have warned against an excessive attachment to the laws of the Church, starting with the Codes, judging them, as a case in point, to be a manifestation of Legalism. As a consequence, hermeneutical paths had been proposed which grant an approach more consonant with the theological foundations and goals, also pastoral, of the canonical norm, leading to a juridical creativity in which a singular situation would become the decisive factor to ascertain the authentic meaning of the legal precept in a concrete case. Mercy, Equity, the *Oikonomia* so dear to the Oriental Tradition, are some of the concepts invoked in such interpretative operations. It is immediately appropriate to note that this framework does not overcome the Positivism which it denounces, limiting itself to substituting it [Positivism] with another in which interpretive human work rises to the level of protagonist in establishing that which is juridical. It lacks the meaning of an objective law which one is to seek, because it remains at the mercy of considerations which claim to be theological or pastoral, but in the end are exposed to the risk of arbitrariness. In such a manner, legal hermeneutics becomes emptied: in the end, it does not take interest in understanding the provision of law, from the moment that it can be dynamically adapted to any whichever solution, even that which is opposed to its letter. Certainly there is in this case a reference to living phenomena, of which, however, one does not grasp the intrinsic juridical dimension.

There exists another way in which the proper understanding of canonical law opens the road to an interpretative work which inserts itself into the search for the truth about the Law and justice in the Church. As I wanted to highlight to the

Federal Parliament of my Country, in the *Reichstag* of Berlin,[3] true law is inseparable from justice. The principle is obviously valid also to the Canon Law, in the sense that it [Canon Law] cannot be shuttered within a merely human system of norms, but must be connected to a just order of the Church, in which a higher law is in effect. Seen through this lens, Human Positive Law loses the primacy which one would want to attribute to it, since law is no longer simply identified with it; in this, however, Human Law is held in value inasmuch as it is an expression of justice, above all for how much it declares as Divine Law, but also for that which it presents as a legitimate determination of Human Law.

In such a manner, a legal hermeneutics which may be authentically juridical is rendered possible, in the sense that, by placing itself in syntony with the very signification of the law, the crucial question can be posed as to what is just in each case. It would be appropriate to observe, in this respect, that in order to grasp the true meaning of the law one must always seize the very reality that is being disciplined, and that not only when the law is primarily declarative of the Divine Law, but also when it constitutively introduces human rules. These are, in fact, to be interpreted also in the light of the reality being regulated, which always contains a nucleus of the Natural Law and the Divine Positive Law, with which every norm must be in harmony in order to be rational and truly juridical.

In such realistic prospectiveness, the interpretative undertaking, at times arduous, takes on meaning and purpose. The use of the interpretive means foreseen by the Code of Canon Law in can. 17, beginning with "the proper meaning of the words considered in their text and context," is no longer a mere logical exercise. It has to do with an assignment that is vivified by an authentic contact with the comprehensive reality of the Church, which allows one to penetrate the true meaning of the letter of the law. Something then occurs, similar to what I said about the inner process of St. Augustine in biblical hermeneutics: "the transcending of the letter has rendered the letter itself credible."[4] In such a manner, also in the hermeneutics of the law is it confirmed that the authentic horizon is that of the juridical truth to love, to seek out and to serve.

It follows that the interpretation of canonical law must take place within the Church. This is not a matter of mere external circumstance, subject to the environs: it is a calling to the same *humus* of Canon Law and the reality regulated by it. *Sentire cum Ecclesia* takes on meaning also within the discipline, by reason of

3 Cf. Discourse to Federal Parliament in the Federal Republic of Germany, 22 September 2011: *L'Osservatore Romano*, 24 September 2011, pp. 6-7.

4 Cf. Post-Synodal Apostolic Exhortation *Verbum Domini*, 30 September 2010, 38: *AAS* 102 (2010), p. 718, n. 38.

the doctrinal foundations that are always present and operative within the legal norms of the Church. In this manner, is also applied to Canon Law that hermeneutics of renewal in continuity of which I spoke in reference to the Second Vatican Council,[5] so closely bound to the current canonical legislation. Christian maturity leads one to love the law ever more and want to understand it and to apply it faithfully.

These foundational approaches are to be applied to all categories of interpretation: from scientific research on Canon Law, to the work of those who labour in the juridical sector in judicial or administrative seats, all the way to the quotidian seeking of just solutions in thc lives of the faithful and of communities. A spirit of docility in welcoming laws is needed, seeking to study with honesty and dedication the juridical tradition of the Church in order to enable oneself to identify with it and also with the legal provisions enacted by Pastors, especially pontifical laws as well as the legal dispositions issued by Pastors, not to mention the Magisterium on canonical questions, which is *per se* binding concerning that which it teaches regarding the Law.[6] Only in this manner may cases be identified in which concrete circumstances require an equitable solution in order to obtain the justice which the general human norm was not able to foresee, and may one be able to exhibit in a spirit of communion what may serve to improve the legislative system.

These reflections acquire a special relevance in the area of laws regarding the constitutive act of Matrimony and its consummation, and the reception of Holy Orders, and of those [laws] pertaining to the respective Processes. Here syntony with the true meaning of the law of the Church becomes a question of broad and profound practical impact on the lives of persons and communities, and it requires special attention. In particular, also to be applied are all juridically binding means which tend to ensure that unity in the interpretation and in the application of laws which is asked for by Justice: the Pontifical Magisterium specifically concerning this area, contained above all within the Allocutions to the Roman Rota; the jurisprudence of the Roman Rota, upon which relevance I have already had the opportunity to speak to you;[7] the Norms and the Declarations issued by other Dicasteries of the Roman Curia. Such hermeneutical unity in that which is essential does not diminish in importance in any way the functions of local tribunals, the first ones called to address complex real situations that are found in every cultural context. Each one of these, in fact, is obliged to proceed with a

5 Cf. Discourse to the Roman Curia, 22 December 2005: *AAS* 98 (2006), pp. 40-53.

6 Cf. John Paul II, Allocution to the Roman Rota, 29 January 2005, 6: *AAS* 97 (2005), pp. 165-166.

7 Cf. Allocution to the Roman Rota, 26 January 2008: *AAS* 100 (2008), pp. 84-88.

sense of true reverence in the presence of the truth regarding the Law, striving to practice in an exemplary manner, in the application of judicial and administrative institutes, communion in discipline, the essential aspect of the unity of the Church.

Bringing myself to the conclusion of this moment of encounter and reflection, I would like to recall the recent innovation — which Bishop Stankiewicz referred to — by virtue of which were transferred to an Office located at this Apostolic Tribunal the competencies for procedures of dispensation from ratified and non-consummated Matrimony and cases concerning the nullity of Sacred Ordination.[8] I am certain that there will be a generous response to this new ecclesial effort.

Encouraging your precious work, which requires faithful, quotidian and strong commitment, I entrust you to the intercession of the Blessed Virgin Mary, *Speculum Iustitiae*, and willingly do I impart my Apostolic Blessing.

8 Cf. Motu Proprio, *Querit Semper*, 30 August 2011: *L'Osservatore Romano*, 28 September 2011, p. 7.

Regolamento della Curia Romana, art. 126 *bis*

Rescripts *Ex Audientia SS.mi*

The text of article 126 bis *of the* General Regulations of the Roman Curia *provides the procedures for a dicastery wishing to request special faculties from the Holy Father. An unofficial English translation is presented, followed by the original Latin.*

UNOFFICIAL ENGLISH TRANSLATION

SECRETARIATE OF STATE

On February 1, 2011 the Holy Father has approved the following text as article 126 *bis* of the *General Regulations of the Roman Curia* (*Regolamento della Curia Romana)*:

"Article 126 *bis* §1. A dicastery which considers it necessary to request special faculties from the Supreme Pontiff must make a request in writing through the Secretariate of State, attaching a draft of the definitive text with a precise indication of the requested faculties, the reason for the request and specifying the eventual derogations of universal or particular canonical norms which would be modified or in some manner are rendered inapplicable.

§2. The Secretariate of State will seek the opinion of the dicasteries that are competent in the matter and those it views as possibly interested in it as well as the Pontifical Council for Legislative Texts as regards the correct juridical formulation and, if it involves any doctrinal questions, the Congregation for the Doctrine of the Faith.

§3. The dossier relative to the special faculties which is to be forwarded to the Supreme Pontiff, analogous to what is provided for in article 126 §3 of the present Regulations (*Regolamento*), will be composed of the request of the dicastery referred to in paragraph 1, the opinions received from the dicasteries referred to in paragraph 2, the possible reformulation of the proposal by the requesting dicastery along with the Report for the Audience (*Foglio d'Udienza*) prepared by the Secretariate of State.

§4. The Secretariate of State will communicate to the dicasteries of the

Roman Curia the text of the faculties possibly granted by the Supreme Pontiff and, along with the requesting dicastery, will determine if and how they are to be publicized."

The Holy Father has ordered the promulgation of the above by its publication in the *Acta Apostolicae Sedis*, determining that it will take effect on March 1, 2011.

Vatican City, February 7, 2011

(signed)
Tarcisio Cardinal Bertone
Secretary of State

SEGRETERIA DI STATO

RESCRITTI "EX AUDIENTIA SS.MI"

II

Il Santo Padre, in data 1 febbraio 2011, ha approvato il seguente testo quale articolo 126 bis del Regolamento Generale della Curia romana:

«Art. 126 bis: §1. Il Dicastero, che ritiene necessario richiedere al Sommo Pontefice speciali facoltà, deve farne domanda per iscritto tramite la Segreteria di Stato, allegando un progetto di testo definitivo, con l'indicazione precisa delle facoltà richieste, la motivazione della domanda e specificando le eventuali deroghe alle norme canoniche universali o particolari, che risulterebbero modificate o in qualche modo disattese.

§2. La Segreteria di Stato richiederà il parere dei Dicasteri competenti in materia e di quelli che ritenga eventualmente interessati, nonché del Pontificio Consiglio per i Testi legislativi per quanto attiene la corretta formulazione giuridica e, se fossero implicate questioni dottrinali, della Congregazione per la Dottrina della Fede.

§3. Il fascicolo relativo alle facoltà speciali, che dovrà essere lasciato al Sommo Pontefice analogamente a quanto previsto nell'art. 126, §3 del presente Regolamento, sarà composto dalla richiesta del Dicastero di cui al §1, dai pareri ricevuti dai Dicasteri di cui al §2, dall'eventuale riformulazione del progetto a cura del Dicastero richiedente, congiuntamente al Foglio d'Udienza a cura della

Segreteria di Stato.

§4. La Segreteria di Stato comunicherà ai Dicasteri della Curia Romana il testo delle facoltà eventualmente concesse dal Sommo Pontefice e, insieme al Dicastero richiedente, valuterà se e come procedere alla sua pubblicazione.»

Il Santo Padre ne ha ordinato la promulgazione tramite la pubblicazione sugli *Acta Apostolicae Sedis*, disponendo che entri in vigore il 1 marzo 2011.

Dal Vaticano, 7 febbraio 2011.

(signed)
Tarcisio card. Bertone
Segretario di Stato

Quaerit Semper

Apostolic Letter
in the form of 'Motu Proprio'

In order to enable the Congregation for Divine Worship and the Discipline of the Sacraments to focus primarily on the promotion of the Sacred Liturgy in the Church, Pope Benedict XVI transferred competence for the dispensation from ratified and non-consummated marriages and for cases concerning the nullity of sacred orders to a newly created Office in the Tribunal of the Roman Rota. The apostolic letter motu proprio *follows.*

Quaerit semper of the Supreme Pontiff Benedict XVI,

with which the Apostolic Constitution *Pastor Bonus* is amended and certain competences transferred from the Congregation for Divine Worship and the Discipline of the Sacraments to the new Office set up at the Tribunal of the Roman Rota for processes of dispensation from ratified and non-consummated marriage and for cases concerning the nullity of sacred ordination.

The Holy See has always sought to adapt its structures of governance to the pastoral needs that arise in the life of the Church in every period of history, thereby modifying the structure and competence of the Dicasteries of the Roman Curia.

The Second Vatican Council moreover confirmed this criterion, reaffirming the need to adapt the Dicasteries to the needs of our time and of different regions and rites, especially with regard to their number, their titles, their competence, their procedures and how they coordinate their activities (cf. Decree *Christus Dominus*, 9).

Following these principles, my Predecessor, Blessed John Paul II, proceeded to an overall reorganization of the Roman Curia through the Apostolic Constitution *Pastor Bonus,* promulgated on 28 June 1988 (*AAS* 80 [1988] 841-930), defining the competence of the different Dicasteries, taking into account the *Code of Canon Law*, promulgated five years earlier, and the norms that were then being drawn up for the Eastern Churches. Later, both my Predecessor and I intervened with further measures, modifying the structure and competence of certain Dicasteries, the better to respond to changed needs.

In present circumstances it has seemed appropriate for the Congregation for Divine Worship and the Discipline of the Sacraments to focus mainly on giving a fresh impetus to promoting the Sacred Liturgy in the Church, in accordance with the renewal that the Second Vatican Council desired, on the basis of the Constitution *Sacrosanctum Concilium.*

I have therefore deemed it opportune to transfer to a new Office, set up at the Tribunal of the Roman Rota, the competence for processes of dispensation from ratified and non-consummated marriage and cases concerning the nullity of sacred ordination.

Consequently, on the advice of the Cardinal Prefect of the Congregation for Divine Worship and the Discipline of the Sacraments and with the favourable opinion of the Dean of the Tribunal of the Roman Rota, having heard the opinion of the Supreme Tribunal of the Apostolic Signatura and of the Pontifical Council for Legislative Texts, I decree the following:

Art. 1

Articles 67 and 68 of the above-mentioned Apostolic Constitution *Pastor Bonus* are abrogated.

Art. 2

Article 126 of the Apostolic Constitution *Pastor Bonus* is amended as follows:

"Article 126 § 1. The Roman Rota is a court of higher instance at the Apostolic See, usually at the appellate stage, with the purpose of safeguarding rights within the Church; it fosters unity of jurisprudence and, by virtue of its own decisions, provides assistance to lower tribunals.

§ 2. An Office has been set up at this Tribunal to examine the fact of non-consummation in a marriage and the existence of a just cause for granting a dispensation. It therefore receives all the acts, together with the *votum* of the Bishop and the remarks of the Defender of the Bond, weighs them according to its own special procedure and, if the case warrants it, submits a petition to the Supreme Pontiff requesting the dispensation.

§ 3. This Office is also competent to examine cases concerning the nullity of sacred ordination, in accordance with both universal and proper law, *congrua congruis referendo.*"

Art. 3

The Office for processes of dispensation from ratified and non-consummated marriage and for cases concerning the nullity of sacred ordination is presided over by the Dean of the Roman Rota, assisted by Officials, Delegated Commissioners and Consultors.

Art. 4

On the day of the entry into force of these regulations, any processes of dispensation from ratified and non-consummated marriage and cases concerning the nullity of sacred ordination still pending at the Congregation for Divine Worship and the Discipline of the Sacraments will be transferred to the new Office at the Tribunal of the Roman Rota and will be decided by the latter.

I order that everything established by this Apostolic Letter *Motu Proprio data* be fully observed in all its parts, notwithstanding anything to the contrary, even if worthy of particular mention, and I establish that it be promulgated through publication in the daily newspaper *L'Osservatore Romano* and that it come into force on 1 October 2011.

Given in Castel Gandolfo, on 30 August in the year 2011, the seventh of my Pontificate.

BENEDICTUS PP. XVI

Advisory Opinions

Introductory Note

The following opinions were assembled by the members of the Publications Advisory Board from among those submitted to the Society for publication. The opinions carry only the weight of the persons named at the end of each opinion. They do not represent the opinion of the diocese or institution to which the author is affiliated nor of the Canon Law Society of America. Advisory opinions are not authentic interpretations of the law, but reflect the scholarly and practical insights of the contributors.

The opinions are arranged according to the canons of the *Code of Canon Law* and the *Code of Canons of the Eastern Churches*. The original questions have been abbreviated or summarized, and the opinions lightly edited to protect the anonymity of the inquirer and to conform to the style of Canon Law Society of America publications.

The Publications Advisory Board expresses gratitude to the canonists who participated in this year's publication. The continued success of this annual project is a result of their willingness to share their time and talent in service to this important work.

The Canon Law Society of America is interested in receiving opinions that members have formulated in response to specific inquiries, and inquiries in need of responses. It also welcomes the participation of members who wish to be involved in this annual project by offering to render opinions to inquiries received by the Board.

Inquiries or contributions may be directed to:

Canon Law Society of America
Office of the Executive Coordinator
3025 Fourth Street, NE
Suite 111
Washington, DC 20017-1102

Canon 11

Baptism and Marriage in the Society of St. Pius X

A case has been referred to the tribunal concerning a couple who have presented themselves for the RCIA in one of our parishes. The man is a Mormon and not validly baptized; the woman was baptized by a priest of the Society of Saint Pius X (SSPX). They were married in the SSPX church. We have two questions. (1) Must she make a profession of faith, as do the Orthodox, when being received into full communion? (2) Is it correct to presume that their marriage was valid, in that neither party was a Catholic at the time of the marriage so they were not bound to the canonical form or impediments of the merely ecclesiastical law?

Opinion

The clergy and faithful of the SSPX are Catholic, albeit in schism.[1] The Apostolic See does not consider the SSPX to be a "church" comparable to the Eastern non-Catholic churches (cf. c. 844 §3) but rather a schismatic movement within the Catholic Church. Consequently, those baptized by a priest of the SSPX are baptized in the Catholic Church (c. 11). Being Catholic, adherents of the SSPX are bound to canon law, including the laws on the impediment of disparity of cult and the canonical form.

Since the bishops and priests of the SSPX are validly ordained, the sacraments celebrated by them requiring only the power of order are valid: confirmation (by a bishop), Eucharist, holy orders, and anointing of the sick. All acts requiring a faculty for validity are invalid in the SSPX, including penance, which requires of the minister the faculty to hear confessions (c. 966), and marriage, which requires the officiant to have the faculty to assist at marriage (cc. 1109-1112). The bishops and pastors of the SSPX do not hold office validly in canon law. Consequently, they lack the power of governance by law. They also lack all faculties of ordinaries and pastors by law and cannot validly delegate any faculties, not only because they do not have any faculties themselves (apart from absolution in danger of death in c. 976), but also because the delegation of a faculty is an act of executive

1 The woman in this case would not have incurred the *latae sententiae* excommunication for schism. See cc. 1364 §1; 1323, 2°; 1324 §1, 9° and §3; Pontifical Council for Legislative Texts, Explanatory Note *Dal motu proprio* on the Excommunication for Schism which the Adherents to the Movement of Archbishop Marcel Lefebvre Incur, 24 August 1996, *Communicationes* 29 (1997) 239-243.

power, which they lack.

So, to answer your first question, the woman is not required to make a profession of faith or be received into full communion, since she already is a Catholic by virtue of her baptism in the Catholic Church. Regarding the second, the marriage of this couple in the SSPX was invalid on two grounds: a defect of canonical form and the impediment of disparity of cult. They married in good faith, however, so their conscience should not be disturbed by informing them that, all along, they were in an invalid union. Therefore, it would be fitting for the local ordinary to grant a *sanatio in radice* (c. 1161). If, however, they are aware that their marriage is invalid, it normally would be preferable to have it convalidated following a dispensation from the impediment (c. 1156 §1). Additionally, it would be advisable to get the woman's baptismal information recorded in the appropriate register of her current Catholic parish. A record of her confirmation by the SSPX bishop (if it occurred) and the eventual *sanatio* or convalidation should also be made. If she has not received confirmation, it should be administered prior to the *sanatio* or convalidation if this can be done without grave inconvenience (c. 1165 §1).

Concerning the validity of this marriage, the outcome would have been different if the woman had been baptized in a non-Catholic church or ecclesial community before joining the SSPX. Such a person remains a non-Catholic since the priests of the SSPX lack the faculty validly to receive a baptized person into the full communion of the Catholic Church (RCIA 481). If such a person, then, were to marry another *baptized* non-Catholic before a priest of the SSPX, the marriage would be valid, provided it was valid in the laws to which the two baptized non-Catholic parties were bound (*Dignitatis connubii*, art. 4, §1). However, if such a baptized non-Catholic, now adhering to the SSPX, were to marry a *non-baptized* person before a priest of the SSPX, the marriage would be invalid due to the impediment of disparity of cult. The bishops of the SSPX, lacking the power of governance, cannot validly grant dispensations.

Dr. John M. Huels, JCD

Canons 119, 1°-2°; 127 §§1, 3; 167; 172 §1, 2°; 220; 625 §1; 627; and 631

Religious Institutes' Use of Information Technology

Canonically, how much possibility is there for using contemporary information technology such as Skype, video phone, or video conferencing in assemblies, chapter, or council decisions?

Opinion

Information technology has made great strides in recent years, offering more and more possibilities for individuals at a distance to be virtually present to one another. Still, it is widely acknowledged that these means are not risk free in terms of confidentiality; canonically, there remains a question of the validity of the acts undertaken. Likewise, such communications, admittedly, are not really quite the same as personal, physical presence. The canonical potential for taking advantage of technology varies with the type of group or college involved, as well as the type of business being transacted. Religious must also be attentive to their proper law, and to values such as quality decision making and confidentiality, which underlie the requirements.

While it may be argued that the code was written before many of these means were available, it remains the current law, upholding the values to be weighed in considering proposals for the future. The code clearly requires the presence of those who are members of a group or college; in the case of formal elections and certain other decisions, this presence is expressly required for the validity of the election or action. On the human level, it is well known that coffee and tea breaks, social gatherings and shared liturgies and prayer, offer invaluable opportunities for a presence that builds relationships and strengthens mutual trust.

Presence and Secrecy in Chapters:

On the matter of presence, canon 119 states norms applicable to all collegial acts, unless statutes provide otherwise. Chapters of religious institutes are, in fact, collegial bodies subject to this norm.

> 1° if it concerns elections, when the majority of those who must be convoked are present, that which is approved by the absolute majority of those present has the force of law;

> 2° if it concerns other affairs, when an absolute majority of those who must be convoked are present, that which is approved by the absolute majority of those present has the force of law;

Each of these paragraphs has further specifications for breaking ties; these normally are either repeated or revised in approved constitutions of religious institutes. Presence, however, is clearly normative, with the computation of a majority based on the number present.

Canon 167 §1 from the section of the code dealing with canonical elections also calls for the presence of the electors. All of these norms are binding for elections in chapters of religious institutes, unless, in certain matters, proper law provides otherwise (c. 164). Canon 625 §1 specifically requires a canonical election for the superior general and that election takes place in general chapter (c. 631 §1).

> When the notice of the convocation has been given legitimately, those present on the day and at the place determined in the same notice have the right to vote. The faculty of voting by letter or proxy is excluded unless the statutes legitimately provide otherwise. (c. 167 §1)

Voting by letter or proxy is not the practice in religious institutes, but special provision is made for those who are in the same house but are unable to be in the chapter hall itself.

> If one of the electors is present in the house where the election occurs but cannot be present at the election due to ill health, his or her written vote is to be sought by the tellers. (c. 167 §2)

An election is invalid if someone is admitted to vote who does not belong to the college or group (c. 169).

Besides actual presence at the time and place of the election, the code requires secrecy (c. 172 §1). While electronic systems have greatly facilitated voting in a chapter room, secrecy of ballots remains an issue in considering the elective function of a chapter whose members are dispersed and wish to vote by email, Skype or video conference. The requirements of presence and secrecy are meant to facilitate the verification of the number of ballots and the inner freedom of each elector. While some stories of illegitimate elections may seem medieval, human nature remains and the stories have contemporary counterparts. More important, however, may be the discreet, interspersed moments of discernment which facilitate the elective process.

Presence and Confidentiality in Council:

In the law on governance in religious institutes, it is required that all superiors have a council whose assistance they must use (c. 627 §1) in accordance with canon 127. This body serves to provide collective wisdom and to curb an autonomous use of authority. Certain acts of superiors require, for validity, either the advice (counsel) or the consent of the council, in accordance with canon 127.

The wording of canon 127, from Book I on juridic acts, is complex, but is critical for the validity of important acts. When universal or proper law calls for the consent of the council, "the college or group must be convoked according to the norm of can. 166..... For such acts to be valid...it is required that the consent of an absolute majority of those present is obtained....." When the law calls for the advice or counsel of the council, the group must be convoked, "unless particular or proper law provides otherwise." In these cases the validity of the acts requires "that the counsel of all is sought."

The last section of the canon emphasizes the necessary transparency of discourse and the necessity of secrecy in important matters.[1]

> All whose consent or counsel is required are obliged to offer their opinion sincerely and, if the gravity of the affair requires it, to observe secrecy diligently; moreover, the superior can insist upon this obligation. (can. 127 §3)

The beginning of the canon makes clear that consent requires a meeting of the council. Universal law requires consent in a number of important matters, largely in protecting the rights and well-being of members and of the institute. These, for example, include granting an indult of departure to a member in temporary vows, granting or seeking the imposition of exclaustration, and the sale or endangering of the patrimonial assets of the institute. Discussion of proposed financial transactions, as well as separation from the institute, can require a high degree of confidentiality. Admission to vows, whether temporary or perpetual, will require either advice or consent, according to proper law (c. 656, 3°; c. 658), but such conversations also require a high degree of confidentiality and discretion.

In the post conciliar period of revising constitutions, many institutes, in the name of greater involvement and participation in governance, wrote and had approved extensive lists of matters requiring the consent of the council. Today,

---

1 It should be noted that canon 127 §2 does not apply to councils, but deals with the advice or consent of *individuals*.

experiencing the difficulty of frequent council meetings, some may wish to consider reducing such lists, taking advantage of canon 127 §1's provision that, for advice, a meeting is not required if such is provided for in proper law. Still, there must be caution regarding confidentiality and a person's right to privacy (c. 220). For example, while the code requires only "hearing the council" in the case of excluding a member from the renewal of vows, the matter would be highly sensitive and confidential (c. 689).

Consequently, while modern technology offers many means of fast and frequent communication, certain cautions must be kept in mind. First, it is, in fact, still the law that collegial bodies such as religious chapters must actually call members together and only those present in the specified time and place may vote. Likewise, for the consent of a council, a meeting is required and the necessary majority for a decision is based on the number present. These requirements may affect the validity of the act. Second, in council, the demands of privacy, confidentiality, and personal reputation may make greater demands on the manner of meeting and/or communicating in concrete cases than is required by the law.

Modern technology can enable broad participation in chapter preparation while remaining in diverse locations, and it can allow observers to be present from a distance when affairs are being discussed by the actual capitulars. Such means could also well serve in the case of congregational assemblies where these are clearly distinct from the chapter. As congregations seek to maximize participation, while economizing on travel in view of both its expense and ecological impact, they have the responsibility to balance such aids with the values of validity and confidentiality.

Sr. Sharon Holland, IHM, JCD

Another Opinion

"Virtual" Meetings in Religious Life

We currently use web conferencing and teleconferencing for our Council meetings and we are considering the use of Skype and other web conferencing and teleconferencing services for our upcoming assembly and for our chapter next year. What are the canonical issues we should be aware of in this matter?

Use of web conferencing and teleconferencing has greatly increased over the past decades as organizations, including religious institutes, seek to reduce cost, travel time, and environmental impact associated with face-to-face meetings. Those who have used these tools successfully have found ways to balance the potential obstacle of decreased interpersonal contact and difficulties relating to the full participation of those present electronically. It is generally helpful to have policies in place that specify:

1. Which meetings can be held by teleconference and which by videoconference,
2. How to verify the identity of participants and speakers,
3. The tools that can be used and how to assure that all participants are able to hear and be heard,
4. How participants will have access to written materials,
5. Whether counsel or consent can be sought at a meeting conducted via teleconference or videoconference, and how this can be verified,
6. How minutes will be taken and/or if the meeting will be recorded.

Assemblies and Chapters

In applying these tools to assemblies and chapters, the same concerns arise, but they are multiplied because of the relatively larger group of persons involved and the longer time for a chapter. Once again, the benefits would include reduced cost, travel time, and environmental impact, and increased participation; the challenges include decreased interpersonal contact and difficulties of full participation of those present electronically.

Parsing canons 631-633 on chapters in religious institutes,[2] we find that chap-

2 Canon 631: "§1 The general chapter, which holds supreme authority in the institute according to the norm of the constitutions, is to be composed in such a way that, representing the entire institute, it becomes a true sign of its unity in charity. It is for the general chapter principally: to protect the patrimony of the institute mentioned in can. 578, promote suitable renewal according to that patrimony, elect the supreme moderator, treat affairs of greater importance, and issue norms which all are bound to obey. §2. The constitutions are to define the composition and extent of the power of a chapter; proper law is to determine further the order to be observed in the celebration of the chapter, especially in what pertains to elections and the manner of handling affairs. §3. According to the norms determined in proper law, not only provinces and local communities, but also any member can freely send wishes and suggestions to a general chapter." Canon 632: "Proper law is to determine accurately what is to pertain to other chapters of the institute and to other similar assemblies, namely, what pertains to their nature, authority, composition, way of proceeding and time of celebration." Canon 633: "§1. Organs of participation or consultation are to fulfill faithfully the function entrusted to them according to the norm of universal and proper law and to express in their own way the concern and participation of all the members for the good of the entire institute or communi-

ters exercise the supreme authority in the institute or, for a provincial chapter, for the province, and that they act according to the norms set out in the constitutions and in proper law. The composition of chapters should "represent the entire institute" as "a true sign of its unity in charity." Thus composed, the chapter is responsible for: 1) protecting the spiritual patrimony of the institute, 2) promoting renewal, 3) electing the supreme moderator, and 4) treating affairs of greater importance and issuing general norms (c. 631 §1). The constitutions are to define the composition and power of the chapter, while the proper law determines the order of celebration, particularly the procedure for election and deliberation (c. 631 §2). Provinces, communities, and members "can freely send wishes and suggestions" to the general chapter (c. 631 §3).

It is for proper law to determine the nature, authority, composition, way of proceeding, and time of celebration of the chapter (c. 632). Other forums of participation (e.g., assemblies or pre-chapter gatherings) should enable the participation of all the members for the good of the entire institute or community.

A chapter is a spiritual event that lasts for days or weeks. In addition to the chapter meetings, it includes liturgy and ritual, prayer, informal gathering, and other means of building the solidarity of the capitular assembly. Unlike other meetings, presence at a chapter or community assembly includes more than hearing and being heard. For this reason, it is hard to imagine how a member of the assembly could fully participate in the entire assembly through electronic means. Since the "way of proceeding" and "manner of handling affairs" is left to proper law, an institute may wish to indicate in its proper law the possibility for the inclusion of "virtual" participants in assemblies and chapters. It would be important that the entire event be planned in order to enable the full participation of members in all aspects of the celebration, including the aesthetic and spiritual elements of the chapter, not only in the meetings and deliberation.

In thinking through the use of teleconferencing at chapters, one could draw an analogy to the participation of various language groups at a chapter, necessitating simultaneous translation. While the translations may be far from perfect, they do allow the participation of members from various language groups and a broader representation from the entire institute (c. 631 §1). Here an effort must be made to ensure that the language groups have adequate opportunity to hear and be heard by others in the chapter. The same situation arises when a member is visually-impaired or hearing-impaired and requires special accommodation

---

ty. §2. In establishing and using these means of participation and consultation, wise discretion is to be observed and their procedures are to conform to the character and purpose of the institute."

to enable him or her to participate in a chapter. On the one hand, the additional voices are valued as a fuller representation of the institute; on the other hand, there are challenges to the full participation of these members. In the same way, use of teleconferencing or videoconferencing may enable a broader participation and better representation of the entire institute, enabling those prohibited from attending to be present electronically.

It may also be possible to incorporate partial participation in an assembly or chapter. This may be accomplished by streaming some presentations or reports from the chapter, or through inviting individuals or groups into dialogue with the capitular assembly for specific purposes. In each of these situations, the electronic participation changes the conversation and influences the outcomes of the chapter.

Possible Ways to Utilize Teleconferencing and Videoconferencing

1. Streaming presentations and reports is a way of allowing the chapter or assembly to share its deliberation with the entire institute or community without a method for those listening to provide any response or interaction. This might be an enhanced way of sending out periodic reports from the chapter or assembly. This helps in one goal of the chapter, namely renewal of the institute; it also helps make the chapter participants more conscious of the various members of the institute for whom and in whose name they are deliberating.
2. Inviting individuals and groups into dialogue with the chapter or assembly through teleconferencing or videoconferencing might be a way of enhancing the reports from different areas or regions of the institute. Those gathered physically at the assembly or chapter are the members of the chapter. Those gathered by teleconference or videoconference are simply given the opportunity to listen to parts of the event and/or to share their particular perspectives or expertise.
3. Another option for use of electronic presence would be in the case of a member of the chapter who is unavoidably absent for some part of the time. For example, if someone is unable to arrive until a day or two after the beginning of the gathering, it may be possible to ameliorate his or her absence by providing teleconferencing for the time of the absence. It is presumed here that the individual would be present for a majority of the chapter and would be able to fully participate in those segments.

In each of these cases, there are several important technical considerations:

- Ensure that the technology is adequate and technical difficulties do not unduly interrupt the flow of the event; have a back-up plan,
- Take reasonable security measures to ensure that proper persons are involved in the teleconference or videoconference and that confidentiality proper to the chapter or assembly be maintained.

In conclusion, teleconferencing and videoconferencing can be used to enhance chapters and assemblies of religious institutes. Participation in the entire event through web conference, teleconference, or videoconference presents significant challenges. If this is to be carried out, these challenges must be foreseen and addressed in the proper law of the institute and in the planning and celebration of the chapter.

Sr. Amy Hereford, CSJ, JCL, JD

Canons 284 §4, 671, and 672

Sister as Guardian for Niece

A sister has approached her major superior with a canonical question: My sister has been working to provide security for my niece as she approaches her 18th birthday. (She will be 17 years old on Aug. 9th!) Since my niece will need guardianship into her adulthood, my sister is seeking to be the primary guardian, of course. I am to be the "Standby Guardian" - meaning that "upon the death, incapacity, renunciation, or removal of the last guardian before me" I would agree to become my niece's legal guardian. Are there any Canonical or Provincial difficulties with this?

Opinion

To make a good decision the leadership of the religious institute in question needs more information. We will mention some details that need to be discovered for a wise response. If we had answers to many of the questions raised in this response, we might be able to revise it in the light of the additional information. For the moment, we can only raise issues.

Short-term commitment

We do not know the parameters of the guardianship this niece will need beyond the age of majority and into her adulthood: how long that might continue, or whether this is a short-term commitment until the niece turns 18 (or 21?). A number of scenarios are possible including a life of several decades for the niece while she remains incapable of assuming charge of her own affairs. Thus the sister could be put in a position of becoming the guardian for many years if the primary guardian could no longer act. That would be like adopting the niece with all of those obligations.

Charity and family bonds may justify a sister becoming a standby guardian but it would be very important to understand all the facts before a woman religious and her religious institute would make such a commitment. If there is adequate financial support for the niece and the commitment would involve about one year, this should be treated with compassion rather than considering strict canonical boundaries.

It would be important to have full disclosure of any court decisions about guardianship and also clear information from the mother of the niece about how she has prepared her daughter for this possibility of guardianship by the aunt.

If there is only about a year before the niece becomes an adult (if, where she resides, the age of majority and adult independence is 18) and if the mother of the girl is currently in good health, there would not be any obvious reason why the religious sister could not accept being named as a potential guardian for such a short time. More consideration would be required if this obligation would extend until the niece becomes 21 meaning this could involve four years of guardianship.

Religious are often named executors of wills by family members, and most religious institutes have no real "canonical" problem with that. The proper law of the religious institute must be considered. The constitutions of the religious institute might have some provision to the contrary, but, usually, such provisions just say that the religious cannot assume such responsibilities without the permission of the competent superior. From what we have been told, the sister would not be placing any community assets at risk, another factor that would have to be considered by the competent authority.

If this is intended as an emergency measure when the intended guardian is unable to function, perhaps a clause could be added to the agreement that the sister would be a temporary guardian while other arrangements are made.

Clarification

The sister and the religious institute need legal clarification of what is meant by guardianship in this particular situation. It would be important for the sister and the religious institute to consider that the apostolic mobility of the sister would likely be limited if this responsibility is a long term commitment.

Living arrangements

Is this niece capable of living independently or would the sister be expected to live with her and take care of her? Are there arrangements in place for assisted living? Is the niece so mentally ill that she might require institutional care? If this young woman needs guardianship after reaching legal majority due to behavioral difficulties or serious illness, that could mean significant emotional and psychological stress for the guardian for many years. Does this niece suffer serious mental illness or is she physically handicapped? Sometimes a person who may be difficult to manage will behave better for a stranger than a family member.

Health care

Would this arrangement include responsibility for health care decisions? Would guardianship include being responsible for those costs? Would the sister, should she become guardian, have durable power of attorney for health care for the niece? Are there provisions to pay for such care?

Financial care

Would guardianship also include the duties which come with a durable power of attorney for financial matters? The sister and the religious institute need to know whether financial responsibility would mean making decisions in regard to whatever financial assets the niece would have or acquire. Is there a substantial trust fund which is adequate for life time care of the niece? If the niece became indigent, would she become the "ward" so to speak of the social benefits system in her country? Needless to say, such a prospect is far from desirable. Has the sister inherited family money she would be expected to use to support the niece should the sister become primary guardian? Perhaps the niece will have good financial provision in the first place so that the guardian's responsibility will be simply of a fiduciary nature in the matter of finances.

If the niece is capable of living alone, perhaps even earning some income, but she is not able to manage her finances, the family might investigate payee programs available through parishes, services for the poor sponsored by religious institutes or Catholic Charities in the area. In a payee program another person is legally designated to manage the finances of someone who cannot handle that.

Canonical issues

The sister has vows of poverty and obedience. She would need the permission of the competent major superior of her institute before assuming this obligation (cc. 671, 672, 284 §4). If the sister belongs to a diocesan institute (c. 672), the competent superior is the local ordinary of the place where the central house or general house of the institute is located.

This guardianship may involve providing for the niece if the primary guardian is deceased or becomes unable to perform the function. In that case, unless the sister has simple vows and permission to use her ample patrimonial funds for this purpose, it would seem the religious institute would have to assume such an obligation. With her vow of poverty the sister remains dependent on her religious institute (c. 600). The religious institute would need to have clear information at what age of the niece the guardian's obligation ceases. As mentioned above, that might be 18 or 21 in most jurisdictions, or this may be an on-going obligation if the niece is unable to assume responsibility for herself despite her chronological age. Before the superior gives permission, the sister should present her with the legal document so the superior will know for what she is giving permission.

If it can be demonstrated that there is no financial obligation on the part of the religious institute, there may be no problem. Family situations such as guardianship for parents especially if the sister is an only child, even managing parental or family finances may seem outside the law but are often permitted if there is no other conflict. The religious institute would need to be alert to potential tax issues if the name of the sister is put on any accounts.

All of these issues would have to be weighed before the competent authorities mentioned in the Code of Canon Law could render a decision regarding the sister's assumption of such a guardianship.

Sr. Victoria Vondenberger, RSM, JCL

Canon 402

Bishops Faculties

Is the faculty to officiate at weddings necessary for a diocesan bishop who resigns and whose resignation is accepted?

Opinion

As canon 1108 §1 states "Only those marriages are valid which are contracted before the local ordinary, pastor, or a priest or deacon delegated by either of them, who assist, and before two witnesses according to the rules expressed in the following canons and without prejudice to the exceptions mentioned in canons 144, 1112, §1, 1116, and 1127, §§1-2." The diocesan bishop is authorized to officiate at weddings throughout the diocese insofar as canon 381 §1 points out: "A diocesan bishop in the diocese entrusted to him has all ordinary, proper, and immediate power which is required for the exercise of his pastoral function except for cases which the law or a decree of the Supreme Pontiff reserves to the supreme authority or to another ecclesiastical authority." Similarly, canon 381 §2 points out that others in charge of particular churches such as a prelate in a prelacy, an abbot in a territorial abbacy, a vicar or prefect apostolic, a diocesan administrator or an apostolic administrator have equivalent powers.[1] The diocesan bishop holds his power personally in virtue of his office.

The diocesan bishop appoints other clerics to the offices of vicar general, episcopal vicar, pastor (*parochus*), and parochial vicar. Any coadjutor bishop is to be appointed as a vicar general and is therefore a local ordinary.[2] Any auxiliary bishop is to be appointed a vicar general or episcopal vicar.[3] The diocesan bishop, vicar general, and the episcopal vicar are local ordinaries and can officiate at weddings throughout the diocese.[4]

1 Canons 368, 370, 371, 134.

2 Canons 406 §1, 134.

3 Canon 406 §2.

4 Canon 134 §1: "In addition to the Roman Pontiff, by the title of ordinary are understood in the law diocesan bishops and others who, even if only temporarily, are placed offer some particular church or a community equivalent to it according to the norm of canon 368 as well as those who possess general ordinary executive power in them, namely, vicars general and episcopal vicars; likewise, for their own members, major superiors of clerical religious institutes of pontifical right and of clerical societies of apostolic life of pontifical right who at least possess ordinary executive

A priest appointed as the pastor of a parish has the faculty to officiate at weddings in that parish. The pastor, however, needs the faculty from a local ordinary or delegation in individual cases from other pastors to officiate at weddings in the diocese outside of his parish's boundaries. The parochial vicar needs the faculty from a local ordinary or delegation from the pastor to officiate at any wedding in a parish.

If they wish to officiate at weddings outside the diocese, all priests need delegation, faculties from a local ordinary in that diocese, or an arrangement whereby faculties are reciprocal between the dioceses. Without any of these authorizations, any marriage at which they officiate would be invalid. For a marriage to be valid it must take place before a duly authorised person and two witnesses.

When a visiting bishop officiates at a wedding outside his own diocese where he is the local Ordinary, even when the bride and groom are from his diocese, the visiting bishop requires proper delegation from the local Ordinary or pastor.[5]

Cardinals cannot officiate at weddings in their Titular churches in Rome without delegation.[6]

Papal nuncios, apostolic Delegates have no authority to officiate at weddings within their jurisdiction, not even in the chapel of the nunciature.[7]

The metropolitan archbishop has no power to officiate at weddings in the dioceses of his suffragen bishops.[8]

When the resignation of a diocesan bishop is accepted by the Holy See, the diocesan bishop does not even have the faculty to officiate at weddings that a pastor has in virtue of his office or from the diocesan faculty *pagella.*

The former diocesan bishop needs the faculty from the new diocesan bishop, diocesan administrator, or apostolic administrator or else delegation in individual cases to officiate validly at weddings in his former diocese.

Rev. Brendan P. Daly, JCD

---

power. §2. By the title of local ordinary are understood all those mentioned in §1 except the superiors of religious institutes and of societies of apostolic life."

5 SRR, *Decisiones*, 30 July 1941, 717-753; SRR, *Decisiones*, 25 May 1942, 408-432; SRR, *Decisiones*, 5 January 1943, 1-15.

6 Canon 357.

7 SRR, *Decisiones*, 28 June 1911. A marriage at which a Papal nuncio had officiated was declared invalid for a lack of canonical form. Cf. also SRR, *Decisiones*, 30 June 1948, 257-267; and 11 June 1949, 287-291.

8 Canon 436.

Canon 580

Aggregation and Covenants

Increasingly, I am contacted by religious institutes that are becoming smaller and are exploring options for their future. Some have considered the possibilities of union or fusion with another institute, some have sought a renewed emphasis on creating a culture of vocation in their communities, some have explored the possibility of fostering new forms of religious life within or aggregated to their institute, or the possibility of developing a group of lay associates imbued with the spirit and charism of their institute. Some institutes have chosen one or more of these options and found them to be a source of renewal and energy for a period of time. Increasingly, however, institutes are asking what their options might be if none of these brings the renewal they had sought and if they now see themselves moving toward the historical fulfillment of their institute's life journey.

Opinion

What options are available to religious institutes that have not chosen union or fusion of their institute with one or more others? I generally propose one of two options: A) aggregating to another institute, which is able to support them as they continue to live faithfully in their last generation, or B) establishing a web of supports and relationships that will help them to move through this phase of their life journey with dignity and leave a legacy worthy of their years of service.

A) Canon 580 states that an institute may aggregate with a more stable institute, without merging canonically. This allows the smaller institute to continue its life for a period of time with the support of the aggregating institute. The aggregating institute is generally a larger, more stable institute that has the resources of time, personnel, and finances to meet its own obligations and is in a position to share these resources with a smaller, less stable institute. Some services that the larger institute can provide are:

1. Ensuring that sponsored ministries receive adequate oversight and/or are transferred to other sponsors.
2. Assisting with the management of assets, investments, and retirement funds of the smaller institute.
3. Assisting in the health-care of members, including permitting members

of the smaller institute to live in the health care facility of the larger institute, and/or overseeing the health-care of members in other facilities.

4. Ensuring that the members participate in government benefit programs and obtain other funding.
5. Oversight of the administration of the smaller institute. This may include an agreement to act as the business and finance office of the smaller institute, or simply overseeing those functions as they are currently in place in the smaller institute. This includes oversight of finance, personnel, and property.
6. Managing the real property of the smaller institute and assisting in the sale of properties that are no longer needed. This may also include allowing use of the larger institute's space for housing and offices.
7. Ensuring that the smaller institute meets its civil and canonical obligations, including assistance in civil and canonical leadership.

A written agreement or covenant between the two institutes, respecting the autonomy of each (c. 580), should set forth the type of assistance that will be provided, along with methods and time-line for the transition into this arrangement, and the compensation that will be provided for these services.

B) The second option for a smaller institute coming to the end of its life is establishing a web of covenants, partnerships, and relationships that will help them move through this phase of their life journey with dignity. Each institute is unique in its history, its culture, its resources, and its relationships and may have unique resources that it can draw on in the final chapters of its life as a community. Examples of partners would be individuals and groups within a local church that have benefited from the services of the religious community or those who have long standing relationships with the institute and would be able to assist in various phases of its life, including retired professionals. This web of relationships meets needs mentioned above for a single covenant relationship. There are four levels of assistance that can be considered:

1. Sponsorship: Ensuring that sponsored ministries receive adequate oversight and/or are transferred to other sponsors.
2. Retirement: Assisting with the management of retirement funds of the institute, overseeing the health-care of members, and ensuring that the members participate in government benefit programs and obtain other funding sources.
3. Administration: Business management, financial administration, and

oversight of personnel and property. Meeting civil obligations of the institute's corporation.

4. Commissarium: Providing assistance in the above categories will allow the institute to maintain its canonical leadership as long as possible before the appointment of a *commissarium* responsible for the canonical leadership of the institute.

An institute's patrimony is its most treasured possession and its greatest gift to the Church, and particularly to the local Church of which it is a part. "This patrimony is comprised of the intentions of the founders, ... the nature, purpose, spirit and character of the institute, and of its sound traditions" (c. 578). It is important that this be preserved to the very end of the life of the institute, even when its members can no longer serve in active ministry. Establishing a web of partnerships and covenants will provide support and assistance to the institute that will allow it to maintain its own autonomy and integrity:

> Can. 586 §1: A true autonomy of life, especially of governance, is recognized for each institute. This autonomy means that each institute has its own discipline in the Church and can preserve whole and entire the patrimony described in can. 578.
>
> §2 Local Ordinaries have the responsibility of preserving and safeguarding this autonomy.

For this reason, the above list is in the order that assistance is most helpful, with a view to preserving the integrity of the institute as long as possible. If matters of sponsorship, health-care, and administration can be attended to by trusted partners and collaborators, the burdens of leadership are lessened and this allows members to remain in canonical leadership for a longer period of time. At the end of the life of the institute however, the institute may seek a *commissarium* or *canonical trustee* to provide leadership during the last phase. As with cases of aggregation, the autonomy of the institute is of utmost importance (c. 580).

Commissarium: A *commissarium* serves the institute and its members and their needs. Like those appointing and electing to offices in religious institutes, the *commissarium* should "have nothing but God and the good of the institute before their eyes" (c. 626). It is wise to select three persons to serve together in this role so that: 1) the group has several competences, 2) there are checks and balances among them, and 3) there is always someone available when a need arises. In addition, those serving in this capacity should be competent and should be disinterested, i.e., they should not be in a position to benefit personally or institutionally from the resources, property, or legacy of the institute. Care should be taken to provide for succession and rotation of the persons serving in this role because it may be required for decades. Finally, some mechanism of accountability should be in place. Though the arrangement must be approved by competent ecclesiastical authority, it is important for an institute itself to provide as much guidance as possible, including nominating the *commissarium* and providing for the relationship between the *commissarium* and others assisting with administration and health-care.

Suppression: Unless determined otherwise by the Apostolic see (c. 584), an institute should not be suppressed until the last member dies or is dispensed. Since it is unthinkable to require elderly religious to seek dispensation from their vows, the institute in which they professed those vows should remain throughout their life. An institute in its canonical life as a juridic person is "by its nature perpetual. It ceases to exist, however, if it is lawfully suppressed by the competent authority, or if it has been inactive for a hundred years" (c. 120). There is no harm in allowing the inactive juridic person with no members to remain as a legacy and testimony to the life and service of the institute until it is extinguished by law after one hundred years.

In my experience, whether an institute chooses to aggregate or covenant with a single religious institute, or to establish a web of relationships, there are several phases in which a canonist familiar with religious life may be able to assist the institute:

1. Information and Education: assisting the institute in exploring options and models and identifying potential partners and relationships.
2. Chapter of Affairs: assisting the institute in choosing a course of action and specifying all the important details and guidelines. This may be the regular chapter or a special chapter convened for this purpose. The course of action often includes a time-line for those changes to be implemented immediately, for intermediate term measures and for the final arrangements.
3. Implementation: assisting the institute in putting documents and agreements in place and responding as the plan unfolds and as questions arise.

Sr. Amy Hereford, CSJ, JD, JCL

Canon 658

Validity of Perpetual Vows

I was recently elected as the superior of a small religious institute. My bishop gave me your phone number and asked me to get your advice about a difficult situation. Less than a year after one of our sisters professed perpetual vows, she was admitted into the psychiatric ward at a local hospital. She has been diagnosed with major depression and has addiction problems. We have never had a situation like this in our community. Since this diagnosis occurred so close to perpetual vows, my council and I wonder if her vows are invalid. If so, what is the next step in this situation? If they are valid, what can be done so that her issues do not affect the entire community?

Opinion

Our conversation provided some very important pieces of information. When this thirty-two year old sister was discerning her vocation, she honestly admitted that she had been sexually abused as a young adult. Even though she had never been in counseling, she thought that she had dealt with this issue in a responsible way. Nevertheless, this woman and the formation director wanted to be certain about this matter. So, she raised this concern during her psychological testing.[1] Since the results did not reveal any psychological illness, everyone assumed that there would not be any future difficulties. Still, psychology has taught us that "one of the most difficult things in life is to gain emotional separateness from that powerful early family environment and not continually repeat it or react against it."[2] Furthermore, "such testing is not predictive of future perseverance in religious life."[3]

After completing a valid novitiate,[4] this sister professed temporary vows. During the next three years, she was very active in the congregation's apostolate and lived with other sisters. Most of the sisters experienced her as a delightful

1 In exercising vigilance about admitting a candidate to the novitiate, canon 642 indicates that a superior may use experts to assess the health, character, and maturity necessary to embrace the particular life of the institute.

2 Ronald Richardson, *Family Ties That Bind* (Bellingham, WA: Counsel Press, 2007) 1.

3 Jordan Hite, "Admission of Candidates and Formation of Members: Canons 641-661" in *A Handbook on Canons 573-746* (Collegeville, MN: The Liturgical Press, 1985) 118.

4 See Canon 643 §1, which lists the impediments to admission to the novitiate.

woman and a person who lived community in a responsible way. Some of them, however, also noticed that she never wanted to talk about her family. She seemed to be very unhappy whenever she went to visit family members. She also started gaining a lot of weight and had some trouble living within her budget. While she enthusiastically participated in community events, she never really had in-depth conversations with any of the members. While the former superior and her council noticed what was transpiring, her ability to live in community and her giftedness for ministering in the congregation's apostolate outweighed the other issues. Therefore, a decision was made to admit her to perpetual vows. Eleven months later, she began spending a lot of time in her room and would not go to work. She made purchases that were way beyond her means. She also continued gaining weight. Eventually, she was taken to the hospital. She has realized that she needs help. Hospital regulations, however, will not permit her to stay there much longer.

At this point, exploring the various facilities that would admit her for long term care is the first priority.[5] In North America there are numerous licensed residential treatment centers.[6] They have a certified professional staff and are accredited. Their evaluation services include psychological, spiritual, and psychosocial components. Their treatment is intensive and interpersonally focused. They also provide aftercare, follow-up services, and they work with a congregation regarding costs. An additional component is a workshop for sisters who are in leadership positions. The seminars provide an understanding of addiction and teach skills regarding how to recognize the signs of addictive behaviors. They also offer leadership an opportunity to discuss any issues related to the recovery of the sister and the way to address the concerns of the other sisters.

From our conversation, it is clear that this sister's perpetual profession is not invalid. There is no external impediment arising from an administrative defect on the part of the former superior (e.g., forgetfulness to obtain some necessary dispensation, error in calculating time, failure to seek the necessary vote of the council, etc.). Furthermore, the sister in question was honest about her background. There was no deceit, grave fear or force at the time of profession. What happened in this situation was a lack of clarity in the early stages of the discernment process about her particular health issue and the ramifications for living consecrated life. With proper treatment it may be possible for this sister to live a

5 Canon 619 speaks about meeting the personal needs of the members in an appropriate manner. One of the keys to exercising this responsibility is the personal relationship between the member and the superior.

6 Many congregations have a list of the places that provide these services.

vowed life in community. She might even become a wounded healer who helps others recover from their addiction.

Dr. Eileen C. Jaramillo, JCL, DMin

CANON 905

DISPENSATION TO CELEBRATE FOUR MASSES ON SUNDAY

I am bishop of a diocese that has a shortage of priests. A priest who celebrates three parish Masses on Sunday morning has asked me to grant him permission to celebrate a fourth Sunday Mass later in the day at a prison. I note that canon 905 of the Code of Canon Law reads *as follows: "§1. It is not licit for a priest to celebrate the Eucharist more than once a day except for certain instances when the law permits such celebration or concelebration more than once. §2. If priests are lacking, the local ordinary may permit priests, for a just cause, to celebrate twice a day and even, if pastoral need requires it, three times on Sundays and holy days of obligation."*

There is no other priest available to celebrate one of the parish Masses or the prison Mass. However, the code does not authorize a local ordinary to permit a priest to celebrate more than three Masses on a Sunday. My question is whether canon 87 would allow me to dispense from this law for the spiritual good of the faithful, or is canon 905 a constitutive law that cannot be dispensed?

OPINION

Often, it is not easy to distinguish merely disciplinary law from constitutive law. Canon 905 has elements of both. On the one hand, it deals with an inherently disciplinary matter, namely, the number of times a day a priest may celebrate or concelebrate Mass. On the other hand, the second paragraph of canon 905 is similar to certain constitutive laws whereby the legislator foresees specific exceptions to the law and provides for them in the law itself, but he does not admit additional exceptions.[1]

In my opinion, this is disciplinary law, but I do not think there can be certainty on this apart from an authentic interpretation. Since the matter is doubtful (c. 14), and in view of general principles of law,[2] you may use your canonical power (cc. 87, 381, 391) to dispense in keeping with the conditions of canon 90: there must

1 See my study, "Categories of Indispensable and Dispensable Laws," *Studia Canonica* 39 (2005) 41-73.

2 "In obscuris minimum est sequendum." "Quoties dubia interpretatio libertatis est, secundum libertatem respondendum erit" (D. [50, 17] 20). "Odia sunt restringenda" (RJ in 6°, 15).

be a just and reasonable cause for the dispensation and you must take account of the circumstances of the case and the importance (*gravitas*) of the law from which the dispensation is given.

Even if canon 905 is a merely disciplinary law, its *gravitas* would indicate that it should not be easily dispensed to the neglect of the values the law seeks to uphold, especially:

- the welfare of the priest, lest his ministry suffer harmful consequences from overwork;[3]
- the welfare of the faithful, lest a priest lack sufficient time to prepare the liturgy and celebrate each Mass reverently, including his promoting the active participation of the faithful;[4]
- assurance that any offerings for subsequent Masses go to the purposes established for this by the Ordinary (c. 951 §1).

The dispensation would be given in a particular case of need, which could include a case with successive application.

Dr. John M. Huels, JCD

---

3 Cf. Congregation for Sacred Rites, Instruction *Eucharisticum mysterium*, no. 26, 25 May 1967, *AAS* 59 (1967) 539-573.

4 Ibid.

Canons 1041, 4°; 1047 §2, 2°; 1049; 1329 §2; and 1398

Candidate for Permanent Diaconate and Abortion

A candidate for ordination to the permanent diaconate in my diocese has acknowledged that he and his former girlfriend decided together to abort their child thirty years prior, before he entered the Catholic Church. He confessed this sin to a Catholic priest before he celebrated the Rite of Reception into the Full Communion of the Catholic Church, and he received absolution at that time. Given that the man was a non-Catholic at the time of the abortion, what issues must be considered before he could be ordained?

Opinion

Sadly, this scenario presents itself with increasing frequency, especially in the United States. This should not be surprising, given recent statistics that indicate twenty-two percent of all pregnancies (excluding miscarriages) in the United States are terminated by abortion.[1]

Canon 1398 states that the procurement of a completed abortion is a canonical delict, punishable by a *latae sententiae* excommunication. Canon 1329 §2 indicates that the same punishment is incurred by those who cooperate in the delict, if the crime would not have been committed without their cooperation. Those otherwise involved may be subject to unspecified *ferendae sententiae* penalties. Needless to say, in all of these cases, before the imposition of any penalty, the general norms of penal law must be considered, including any mitigating or aggravating factors (cc. 1323-1327). In the scenario presented, however, the man was not a Catholic at the time of the abortion. Therefore, while the act was morally evil, it would not constitute a canonical delict (cc. 1 and 11).

As to whether the man is irregular for the reception of orders, canon 1041, 4° places in this category all those who have procured an abortion or positively (i.e., actively) cooperated in the procurement of an abortion. Since this law places a restriction upon who may receive ordination, it must be interpreted strictly (c. 18). For example, someone who voted for a candidate for public office who did not embrace an anti-abortion platform would not incur this irregularity, since

1 R.K. Jones and K. Kooistra, "Abortion incidence and access to services in the United States," *Perspectives on Sexual and Reproductive Health*, 43:1 (2011) 41-50.

such voting would not be considered positive cooperation. In the case presented, while it would be wise to explore precisely what the man means in describing his direct involvement with his former girlfriend, his statement that he and his girl friend decided together to abort their child points in the direction of sufficient involvement on his part to have incurred the irregularity. Other actions that may be considered positive cooperation include paying for the abortion and coercing the mother to have the procedure.[2]

The fact that the man was not a Catholic when the abortion took place does not exempt him from the irregularity, since abortion is a grave offense against the divine law. Therefore, it has juridic effects for non-Catholics who later become Catholic, in much the way that a valid natural marriage constitutes an impediment to a future union.

In deciding whether or not to seek a dispensation from the irregularity, the diocesan bishop will need to weigh several factors alongside the man's overall suitability for ordination. These include the length of time since the abortion, whether the man appreciates the gravity of the abortion and has suitable contrition, and whether or not the man participated in more than one abortion. If there is meaningful doubt about the man's level of involvement in any particular abortion, the dispensation may be requested *ad cautelam*.

The authority to dispense from the irregularity belongs to the Apostolic See (c. 1047 §2, 2°). If the abortion is occult, the Apostolic Penitentiary has competence. If not, the petition for dispensation is directed to the Congregation for Divine Worship and the Discipline of the Sacraments. In either case, the number of abortions at issue must be stated for the validity of the dispensation (c. 1049 §2), as the irregularity is multiplied by the number of abortions (c. 1046).

Customarily, a timely dispensation is forthcoming in light of a favorable *votum* from the appropriate ecclesiastical authority, coupled with the assurance that no scandal will result from the granting of the dispensation. However, it is important to note that the decision whether or not to ordain the man still rests with the diocesan bishop.

Should the deacon later seek ordination to the priesthood, there is no need to secure another dispensation (c. 1049 §3).

If the candidate for ordination belongs to a religious institute, his major su-

2 See Robert J. Geisinger, Commentary on Canon 1041, *New Commentary on the Code of Canon Law,* John Beal et al., eds. (New York/Mahwah: Paulist Press, 2000) 1217-1218 on voluntary, active, and effective participation.

perior would petition the Congregation for Institutes of Consecrated Life and Societies of Apostolic Life for a dispensation from the irregularity in non-occult cases. The Apostolic Penitentiary, however, remains competent for occult matters, even in regard to religious. One question to consider in cases involving a religious relates to when to request the dispensation. If it is sought too early (i.e., when the man is only a novice), it is too soon in his journey with the community to determine whether or not he will ever be a candidate for ordination. Yet, a delay may result in a man's spending many years in formation in anticipation of ordination in a particular institute, only to find himself subject to a new superior who is unwilling to request a dispensation from this particular irregularity.

Ms. Amy Strickland, JCL

Canons 1086 §1 and 1117

Validity of Marriage

I understand that Pope Benedict made some changes to the Code of Canon Law. Do these changes affect the validity of marriage?

Opinion

In the Apostolic Letter *Omnium in mentem*, Pope Benedict XVI modified five canons of the Code of Canon Law: 1008; 1009; 1086 §1; 1117; and 1124. These changes became effective on April 9, 2010.

The changes to canons 1086 §1 and 1117 have a significant impact on whether a marriage might be null due to a lack of canonical form or due to an impediment. First, we will provide some background to these canons as initially promulgated in the 1983 code and the difficulties in applying them that led to the changes. Next, we will discuss the changes to these canons. Finally, we will provide a timeline to clarify whether and when Catholics who defect from the Church are or are not bound by canonical form and disparity of cult.

Background

Prior to the 1983 code, Catholics who "left the Church" were still bound by the canonical form of marriage and the impediment of disparity of cult (i.e., the marriage between a Catholic and a non-baptized person). This was changed in 1983 when canons 1086 §1 and 1117 of the 1983 Code of Canon Law exempted those who formally defected from the Catholic Church from the impediment of disparity of cult and the canonical form of marriage. They were still bound, however, by all other ecclesiastical laws.

These provisions of the code helped to avoid the invalid celebration of marriages by persons who defected from the Catholic Church. Since the promulgation of the 1983 code, however, the application of these same provisions has raised some significant questions and problems. For example, what does it mean to leave the Church by a formal act? How does one determine when that has happened?

On March 13, 2006, the Pontifical Council for Legislative Texts (PCLT) clarified what it meant to defect from the Catholic Church by a formal act. It stated that leaving the Church by a formal act requires that one *decide interiorly* to leave the Church. In addition, one must *manifest that decision exteriorly* in a valid juridical act. Finally, that decision must be *received* by the competent ecclesiastical authority. One must communicate that act of defection in writing to one's ordinary or proper pastor.

There has been some debate whether this circular letter from the PCLT is retroactive or prospective.[1] In our opinion, it is *prospective* because the requirement to communicate the defection to the competent ecclesiastical authority in writing goes beyond the sense of the words of the law that are certain in themselves (cf. c. 16).

Since the circular letter is not retroactive, one must have some criteria to determine whether someone left the Catholic Church by a formal act *prior to March 13, 2006*. We propose that such a determination can be made if the person has decided interiorly to leave the Church and manifested that decision exteriorly. There must be both the *interior* act of the will to depart and an *exterior* act to manifest that decision. For example, one rejects one or more doctrines of the Catholic faith and joins another Christian denomination. A departure from the Catholic Church by a formal act takes place when someone commits the delict of apostasy, heresy, or schism (cf. cc. 751, 1364 §1). The mere failure to practice one's faith or "church-hopping" to find something "meaningful" do not constitute the departure by a formal act, for they do not manifest an interior decision to *leave* the Catholic Church.

The Changes and Their Rationale

The PCLT studied the matter and consulted bishops throughout the world. The PCLT sought to gather information regarding the praxis of the implementation of the provisions of the code to prevent the invalid celebration of marriage for those who had left the Church by a formal act. In addition, the PCLT looked for any difficulties associated with the implementation of these provisions.

In particular, it was found that these provisions made it more difficult for fallen away Catholics to return to the Church and enter a new marriage if a previous

1 See Ludger Müller, "Die Defektionsklauseln im kanonischen Kirchenrecht. Zum Schreiben des Päpstlichen Rates für Gesetzestexte an die Vorsitzenden der Bischofskonferenzen vom 13. März 2006," *Archiv für katholisches Kirchenrecht* 175 (2006) 383; Marcus Nelles, "Der Kirchenaustritt – kein 'actus formalis defectionis'," *Archiv für katholisches Kirchenrecht* 175 (2006) 360; Bruno Primetshofer, "Der Kirchenaustritt und seine rechtlichen Folgen," *Theologischpraktische Quartalschrift* 156 (2008) 35; Hartmut Zapp, "'Kirchenaustritt' zur Vermeidung von Kirchensteuern – nun ohne kirchenrechtliche Konsequenzen," in *Dienst an Glaube und Recht. Festschrift für Georg May zum 80. Geburtstag*, Anna Egler and Wilhelm Rees, eds. (Berlin: Duncker & Humblot, 2006) 83.

marriage had failed. For example, Joe leaves the Catholic Church and marries Sue in a Protestant celebration. Then some time later that marriage breaks up. After a time, he meets Beth, a Catholic, who helps him rediscover his Catholic faith. Joe wants to return to the Church and marry Beth. In this case, he would have to obtain a declaration of nullity of his previous marriage to Sue, which may or may not be granted depending upon whether grounds for nullity can be proven. This makes his return to the Church more difficult.

For this and other reasons, the Holy Father decided to strike the provisions that one is not bound to canonical form and disparity of cult if one defects from the Church by a formal act. Therefore, effective April 9, 2010, Catholics who have left the Catholic Church by a formal act are still bound by the canonical form of marriage and the impediment of disparity of cult.

A Timeline for when Catholics who defect are or are not bound by canonical form and disparity of cult

A. Canonical Form

- Catholics who left the Church and married outside the Church *prior to November 27, 1983* were bound by canonical form. Therefore, their marriage is invalid due to lack of canonical form.
- Catholics who left the Church by a formal act and married outside of the Church *on or after November 27, 1983* but *before March 13, 2006*, were not bound by the canonical form of marriage. Therefore, their marriage is presumed valid. Such a case would require the full declaration of nullity process.
- Catholics who left the Church by a formal act and married outside of the Church *on or after March 13, 2006 but before April 9, 2010* were not bound by the canonical form of marriage only if they left the Church in the manner specified by the Pontifical Council for Legislative Texts. Therefore, their marriage is presumed valid. Such a case would require the full declaration of nullity process.
- Catholics who left the Church and married outside the Church *on or after April 9, 2010* were bound by canonical form. Therefore, their marriage is invalid due to lack of canonical form.

B. Disparity of Cult

- Catholics who left the Church and married a non-baptized person outside the Church *prior to November 27, 1983* were bound by the impediment of disparity of cult. Therefore, their marriage is invalid due to an impediment. Such a case could be processed as a documentary case to show the existence of the impediment. It should be noted that in this case the marriage would be invalid for two reasons, the impediment of disparity of cult and lack of canonical form. While in theory it is possible to establish invalidity due to the impediment, in practice it would usually be easier to establish invalidity due to lack of canonical form.

- Catholics who left the Church by a formal act and married a non-baptized person outside of the Church *on or after November 27, 1983* but *before March 13, 2006*, were not bound by the impediment of disparity of cult. Therefore, their marriage is presumed valid. Such a case would require the full declaration of nullity process.
- Catholics who left the Church by a formal act and married a non-baptized person outside of the Church *on or after March 13, 2006 but before April 9, 2010* were not bound by the impediment of disparity of cult only if they left the Church in the manner specified by the Pontifical Council for Legislative Texts. Therefore, their marriage is presumed valid. Such a case would require the full declaration of nullity process.
- Catholics who left the Church and married a non-baptized person outside the Church *on or after April 9, 2010* were bound by the impediment of disparity of cult. Therefore, their marriage is invalid due to an impediment. Such a case could be processed as a documentary case to show the existence of the impediment. It should be noted that in this case the marriage would be invalid for two reasons, the impediment of disparity of cult and lack of canonical form. While in theory it is possible to establish invalidity due to the impediment, in practice it would usually be easier to establish invalidity due to lack of canonical form.

Rev. John F. Doerfler, STD, JCL
Ms. Daniela Knepper, JCL

Canon 1190

The Sale of Sacred Relics

Online auction sites, like eBay, frequently list relics for sale. Although these relics are very small, vendors regularly confirm that they are "blessed" and "authentic." Is it permitted to sell or purchase these relics? If not, what can be done about this practice?

Opinion

Relics are traditionally classified in three classes. *First class* relics consist of items directly related to the life of Christ or the bodily remains of the saints. *Second class* relics refer to items frequently used or worn by a saint (e.g., a religious habit or cassock). *Third class* relics include items that have come into contact with a first or second class relic.[1] Although these terms are not used in the *ius vigens*, this form of classification of relics is reflected in the *Directory on Popular Piety and the Liturgy*, n. 236.

> The term 'relics of the Saints' principally signifies the bodies - or notable parts of the bodies - of the Saints who, as distinguished members of Christ's mystical Body and as Temples of the Holy Spirit (cf. 1 Cor 3, 16; 6, 19; 2 Cor 6, 16) in virtue of their heroic sanctity, now dwell in Heaven, but who once lived on earth. Objects which belonged to the Saints, such as personal objects, clothes and manuscripts are also considered relics, as are objects which have touched their bodies or tombs such as oils, cloths, and images.[2]

A different form of classification has been adopted by the Apostolic Sacristy. In addition to conserving a relic of the holy Cross, the Apostolic Sacristy conserves the relics of saints, which are classified as follows: relics *ex ossibus* (of bones); relics *ex carne* (of flesh); and relics *ex indumentis* (of apparel).[3]

---

1 E.A. Dooley, *Church Law on Sacred Relics*, Canon Law Studies, n. 70 (Washington, DC: Catholic University of America, 1931) 4.

2 Congregation for Divine Worship and the Discipline of the Sacraments, *Directory on Popular Piety and the Liturgy: Principles and Guidelines*, December 17, 2001 (Vatican City: *Libreria Editrice Vaticana*, 2002).

3 Office for the Liturgical Celebrations of the Supreme Pontiff, "Norms for the concession of relics from the Apostolic Sacristy," February 15, 1994: *Notitiae* 30 (1994) 348-350; English translation in *CLD* 13: 578-579.

The 1983 code forbids the sale of all types of relics, utilizing extraordinarily strong language: *nefas est* (c. 1190 §1).[4] This pertains to all relics, including those in the possession of individual members of the faithful. The prohibition on the sale of relics does not preclude, however, individuals or organizations from requesting a monetary contribution to offset postage costs or other related expenses, such as the cost of containers in which the relics are preserved or displayed. The terms of the exchange should be clearly identified from the outset so as to remove all appearance of trafficking in sacred relics.[5]

The 1917 Code of Canon Law contained provisions that are no longer found in the 1983 code. Local Ordinaries, vicars forane, pastors, and others having the care of souls were instructed to take great care to prevent relics, especially of the most holy Cross, from being sold and thus passing into the possession of non-Catholics (*CIC*/17, c. 1289 §1). Rectors of churches were to ensure that sacred relics were in no way profaned, lost by negligent people, or not preserved respectfully (*CIC*/17, c. 1289 §2). Furthermore, a *latae sententiae* excommunication, reserved to the Ordinary, was incurred by those who manufactured or knowingly sold, distributed, or exposed for public veneration *false* relics (*CIC*/17, c. 2326). Despite the absence of these and other provisions from the 1983 code, care must always be taken to ensure the dignified preservation of sacred relics, lest they be disposed of in a disrespectful manner or sold without any consideration of their sacredness or importance.

In addition to forbidding the sale of sacred relics, the 1983 code also indicates that relics of great significance and other relics honored with great reverence by the people may not be validly alienated (see cc. 1291-1296) or transferred on a permanent basis without the permission of the Apostolic See (c. 1190 §2).[6] Such relics are considered ecclesiastical goods (cf. c. 1257 §1). Consequently, one who alienates such relics without the permission of the Apostolic See is to be punished with a just penalty (c. 1377). The Congregation for the Causes of Saints has competence to decide everything concerning the authentication of holy relics and their preservation (*Pastor bonus*, art. 74), yet the Congregation for Divine

4 The term *nefas est* is used only four times in the *Code of Canon Law*, forbidding (1) the consecration of one matter without the other or even both outside the Eucharistic celebration (c. 927); (2) the violation of the seal of confession (c. 983 §1); (3) forcing anyone in any way or for any reason to receive Holy Orders (c. 1026); and (4) the sale of relics (c. 1190 §1). Interestingly, all four uses are found in Book IV.

5 See Dooley, 109.

6 Relics of great significance include: the body, the head, the arm, the forearm, the heart, the tongue, the hand, the foot, or that part of the body on which the martyr has suffered, provided it is entire and not too small (cf. c. 1281 §2 of the 1917 Code).

Worship and the Discipline of the Sacraments has competence concerning the cult of sacred relics (*Pastor bonus*, art. 69).

One should be especially suspicious of vendors' claims of authenticity. Although norms exist to verify the authenticity of relics,[7] it is not inconceivable for unscrupulous vendors to fabricate or falsify documents, especially in a language unknown to prospective buyers. Despite the intrinsic value of authentic relics, it remains absolutely forbidden to sell them (c. 1190 §1). Similarly, any claim that relics have been blessed is particularly problematic. Relics require no additional blessing, and it has never been the practice of the Church to impart a blessing on sacred relics.[8]

What can be done to halt or reduce the online sale of relics? On the one hand, the faithful could be encouraged to purchase these relics to ensure that they are rescued from public auction and all inappropriate uses; on the other hand, these transactions only encourage the trafficking of relics, particularly if the faithful engage in some form of competitive bidding process that results in a higher purchasing price. In the past, the Holy See has forbidden the purchasing of relics even for the good purpose of rescuing them from public sale. Instead, the local Ordinary was to be informed.[9] Earlier commentators argued, however, that simony – the attempt to buy or sell for a temporal price something that is spiritual or connected to spiritual things (cf. *CIC*/17, c. 727) – was not committed when relics were purchased to rescue them from *imminent* danger of profanation, if there was insufficient time to consult the Ordinary.[10]

---

7 Specific instructions, for instance, have been provided for the canonical recognition of the mortal remains of a Servant of God in an appendix to Congregation for the Causes of Saints, Instruction for conducting diocesan or eparchial inquiries in the causes of saints *Sanctorum Mater*, May 17, 2007 (Rome: Congregatio de Causis Sanctorum, 2007) 95-99.

8 Reliquaries, the containers in which sacred relics are preserved and displayed, may be blessed. The *Book of Blessings* contains no specific formula of blessing, but the order for blessing articles for liturgical use may be appropriately used (*Ordo benedictionis rerum quae in liturgicis celebrationibus usurpantur*, in *De benedictionibus*, editio typica, May 31, 1984 [Vatican City: Typis Polyglottis Vaticanis, 1984] 409-413). The earlier *RitualeRomanum* contained a specific blessing for reliquaries, and in light of the instruction *Universae Ecclesiae*, art. 25, this liturgical book may be utilized for such purposes (*Rituale Romanum Pauli V Pontificis Maximi iussu editum aliorumque Pontificum cura recognitum atque ad normam Codicis Iuris Canonici accommodatum, SS.mi D.N. Pii Papae XII auctoritate ordinatum et auctum*, Typis Polyglottis Vaticanis, 1952, Titulus IX, Caput IX, n. 8).

9 See Congregatio Indulgentiarum et Reliquiarum, Decree, 21 December 1878, in *Decreta authentica Sacrae Congregationis indulgentiis sacrisque reliquiis praepositae ab anno 1668 ad annum 1882* (Ratisbonae: F. Pustet, 1883) 405, n. 443.

10 See E. Génicot, *Institutiones Theologiae Moralis*, 2 vols. (Bruxelles: Édition Universelle, 1951) vol. 1, p. 228, n. 288; G. Cocchi, *Commentarium in Codicem Iuris Canonici ad usum scholarum*, 8 vols. (Taurinorum Augustae, Marietti, 1942) vol. 5, 224. Abbo and Hannan argued that "in an urgent case, one is justified in redeeming the relics even by offering the price necessary to do so,

With the sophistication of online commerce, where the parties to the transaction are unknown to one another, it is unclear how the abovementioned solutions can be satisfactorily invoked in regard to relics discovered at an online auction site. An intervention by the local Ordinary is likely to achieve little, even, perhaps, inadvertently increasing the value of the relic by drawing attention to the online auction. Similarly, avoiding the appearance of simony and the trafficking of relics is a herculean task – even in imminent danger of profanation – that is more likely to be honored in the breach than in the observance. It would seem, then, that the most effective resolution of this matter is *preventative* rather than *restorative*: the faithful are to be made aware of the absolute prohibition on the sale of relics, while the competent ecclesiastical authorities are to scrupulously provide for the reverent preservation, permanent transfer, and valid alienation of the same.

Dr. Chad J. Glendinning, JCD

---

presuming in the circumstances the requisite authorization of the local ordinary" (J.A. Abbo and J.D. Hannan, *The Sacred Canons*, 2 vols. [St. Louis, MO: B. Herder Book Co., 1960] vol. 2, 534).

Canon 1267

Restricted Donations to a Parish

Our parish church, school, and rectory are in need of significant repairs. A well-intended parishioner recently told our pastor that, from now on, she will only give donations for "special purposes" to the parish (e.g., for the repair of the church roof). She believes that giving such "restricted donations" will assure that they remain with the parish. She wants nothing of her donations to reach the diocese or to be subject to the annual diocesan tax. Can the pastor accept such gifts? If so, must they be reported as "ordinary parish income"? And would they be subject to the diocesan tax, or not?

Opinion

Any consideration of an answer to these questions necessarily begins with canon 1267, which states:

> §1. Unless the contrary is established, offerings given to superiors or administrators of any ecclesiastical juridic person, even a private one, are presumed given to the juridic person itself.
>
> §2. The offerings mentioned in §1 cannot be refused except for a just cause and, in matters of greater importance if it concerns a public juridic person, with the permission of the ordinary; the permission of the same ordinary is required to accept offerings burdened by a modal obligation or condition, without prejudice to the prescript of can. 1295.
>
> §3. Offerings given by the faithful for a certain purpose can be applied only for that same purpose.

As this canon is applied to a parish (a public juridic person: see c. 515 §3) whose administrator is its *parochus* (see c. 532): offerings given to the *parochus* are presumed to belong to the parish, and are to be used according to the intention of the donor. Furthermore, certain norms apply both for the *refusal* and the *acceptance* of offerings to the parish:

1. offerings can be refused by the *parochus* – for a just cause
2. offerings "of greater importance" can be refused by the *parochus* – also

for a just cause, but with the permission of the local ordinary (who obviously must also agree that there is a just cause to refuse the gift)

3. offerings which carry a "modal obligation" or "condition" can be accepted by the *parochus* – but *only* with the permission of the local ordinary

A "modal obligation" attached to an offering imposes a requirement on the recipient but, if the requirement is not fulfilled, the recipient retains the gift. A "condition" attached to an offering imposes a requirement and, if the requirement is not fulfilled, the gift returns to the donor.

In the case at hand, inasmuch as the parishioner intends her donations for specific purposes, she has attached a modal obligation to them. They are to be used only for a specific purpose. Therefore, before the *parochus* can accept these offerings, he must receive the permission of the local ordinary. If the local ordinary grants this permission, the donations must be used for the intended purpose (and, also in keeping with the intention of the donor, they would not be subject to the diocesan tax). If the local ordinary refuses to grant this permission, the *parochus* cannot accept the gift.

The *parochus* will need to explain to the donor that he must have the permission of the local ordinary before accepting her gift. During this dialogue with the donor, the *parochus* may take the occasion to explain that general revenue is needed to operate the parish, and that one of the routine costs of this operation is paying the diocesan tax. While "no one likes to pay taxes," such payment is a routine part of life, civil and ecclesiastical. The parish is a part of the larger Catholic community, the diocese, which also needs sufficient means to perform its many works; much of the operating revenue of the diocese is generated by the moderate tax imposed on parishes.

Also, if the offering is intended for "major" repairs to parish buildings, such repairs may well have been identified as parochial acts of extraordinary administration by diocesan particular law (see c. 1281 §2). In such a case, the *parochus* will need the written faculty of the local ordinary before he performs such acts validly (c. 1281 §1).

To avoid the difficult situation posed in the above question in the future, the diocesan bishop may wish to exclude from "taxable" income certain previously approved unique initiatives in parishes – for example, revenues generated by fund-raising appeals (c. 1262) or special collections (c. 1266) in order to fund major repairs. To conduct such initiatives, the law requires the *parochus* to obtain the prior permission of the local ordinary. The monies generated would not be subject to the diocesan tax because the diocesan formulary would exclude them (see c. 1263).[1]

Finally, it will be helpful for the local ordinary to issue special instructions (c. 1276 §2) addressing the acceptance of restricted donations, including restricted gifts for parochial acts of extraordinary administration, in order to assist the *parochus* in handling such donations appropriately.

Rev. Msgr. John Renken, STD, JCD

1 Certainly, to "tax" monies generated for approved extraordinary parochial projects does nothing to promote good will among parishioners. For example, if a project costs $100,000 and superimposed on this is a 10% tax, in order to accomplish the extraordinary parish project, the parish must generate $111,000. Arguably, it is such taxing of unique projects that contributes to prompting parishioners (and *parochi*) to seek ways to generate parish revenue without the knowledge of diocesan authorities. Nobody wins.

Canon 1379

A Simulation of the Precious Blood in a Eucharistic Celebration

A large Catholic shrine in my city serves tourists and the local population. Communion under both Species is offered at most Masses there. At Communion time, however, off to one side of the sanctuary, a minister also offers "special wine" from a chalice. It is grape juice. When I asked about this practice, I was told by a staff member that a number of alcoholics attend Mass at the Shrine and that they cannot drink the "Blessed Wine" from Mass. I suggested that this practice amounted to faking a sacrament, and was told that everyone knows about it so there is no deception involved. Please comment.

Opinion

There are, I think, three distinct problems presented here, the most serious being the possible delict of sacramental simulation. Before discussing that possibility, however, I will address briefly two other problems, namely, the intrusion of a 'blessed grape juice distribution rite' into the Mass and the staff member's inaccurate presentation of Eucharistic doctrine.[1]

The use of the term "blessed wine" can be misleading. After a priest duly pronounces the words of consecration over valid matter, there is no longer present on the altar "bread" and "wine" of any sort; there is present only the Body, Blood, Soul, and Divinity of Christ under two Species (*CCC* 1373-1381, 1413). To describe the Precious Blood as "blessed wine" is, strictly speaking, to express a material heresy. But whatever the etiology of the assertion that Catholics receive "blessed wine" at Communion time, such a description should be corrected, especially when it is encountered among staff members at an important Catholic shrine.

1 A possible fourth issue is whether the practice could be viewed as an instance of the approved use of *mustum* at Mass. It would not be so excused, for three reasons: first, there is no indication that the grape juice was the object of the celebrant's consecratory intention; second, almost all instances of the approved use of *mustum* deal with an alcoholic *priest's* celebration of Mass; third, specific authorization is required before any non-celebrant may take *mustum* and such authorizations are granted only to persons who cannot take even the Host. See John Huels, commenting on canon 924, in J. Beal, et al., eds., *New Commentary on the Code of Canon Law*, (New York/ Mahwah: Paulist Press, 2000) 1117; and James Provost, "Canons 924 and 29-34" in K. Vann, *et al.*, eds., *Roman Replies and CLSA Advisory Opinions 1995* (Washington, DC: Canon Law Society of America, 1995) 75-80, 78.

Further, the introduction of a rite of administering blessed grape juice to certain faithful during Mass, regardless of what might be said about simulation, is a violation of canon 846 §1.[2] The words used and/or rites applied during the sacred liturgy must be approved by the Apostolic See or diocesan bishop per canon 838 §1,[3] but no rite for the distribution of blessed grape juice exists in the *Missale Romanum* (2002), nor am I aware of any bishop's having authorized the introduction of such a rite into Mass. On grounds of liturgical integrity alone, then, this 'grape juice distribution rite' should cease, lest the sign value of the liturgy in regard to the *unity* of the Church be damaged (c. 837 §1) and the faithful's fundamental right to worship God "according to the prescripts of their own rite" (c. 214) be threatened.

At this point, we must consider the possibility that the described practice is a canonical delict.

Simulation of a sacrament is prohibited by canon 1379, which states: "In addition to the cases mentioned in can. 1378, a person who simulates the administration of a sacrament is to be punished with a just penalty." Canon 1379 is new with the 1983 code and commentary on it has been light.

Antonio Calabrese has claimed that the only form of sacramental simulation punished by canon law is the pseudo-*celebration* of a sacrament–not the administration of a fictitious sacrament such as would occur, for example, when unconsecrated hosts are distributed at Mass.[4] Calabrese is directly answered, however, by Ángel Marzoa, who holds that simulation "may be committed... by anyone pretending to administer/distribute the Eucharist with hosts that are not consecrated," explaining that this interpretation "is supported by the habitual differentiation that the [1983 code] posits between 'consecrate/celebrate' and

2 1983 *CIC,* canon 846 § 1: "In celebrating the sacraments the liturgical books approved by competent authority are to be observed faithfully; accordingly, no one is to add, omit, or alter anything in them on one's own authority."

3 1983 *CIC*, canon 838 § 1: "The direction of the sacred liturgy depends solely on the authority of the Church which resides in the Apostolic See and, according to the norm of law, the diocesan bishop."

4 "Per amministrazione di sacramento è qui intesa l'azione o rito che produce quel sacramento.... Chi distribuisce consapevolmente ostie non consecrate, commette un peccato gravissimo ma non il delitto punito da questo canone." Antonio Calabrese, *Diritto Penale Canonico* (Edizioni Paoline, 1990) 239-240. Calabrese is joined, without elaboration, by William Woestman, who holds that "it would be a most grave sin for a cleric or lay person to distribute knowingly unconsecrated hosts to those seeking holy Communion" and adds that "the ordinary could punish such an offense in virtue of c. 1399" *Ecclesiastical Sanctions and the Penal Process* (Ottawa: St. Paul's University, 2000) 119. But if Marzoa, discussed below, is correct (and I think he is) there is no need to invoke canon 1399 against those simulating the distribution of the Precious Blood as described in our case.

'administer' the Eucharist (cf., e.g., cc. 910, 917-919, 923, 929, 931), likewise in the denomination as 'ministers' those who distribute holy Communion (c. 910)."[5] The great sacramental lawyer Felix Cappello expressly recognized the distinction between *confection* of a sacrament and *administration* of a sacrament; given the fact that 1917 *CIC*, c. 2322, 1° penalized only the confection (*celebrationem*) of the Eucharist, Cappello held that mere administrators of fictitious hosts, despite their committing a grievously sinful act, were not canonically liable as simulators.[6] Of course, canon 1379 now expressly reaches those who simulate even the "administration" of a sacrament and therefore one cannot but agree with Marzoa that canon 1379 threatens punishment against those who engage in the *administration* of fictitious sacraments.

That said, however, the assertion by the shrine staff member that "everyone knows about the practice so there is no deception involved" raises a different point that needs careful consideration.

Commentators on simulation in regard to the Eucharist in the 1917 Code (*CIC* c. 2322) noted that what might *appear* to be simulation was not simulation when there was no possibility that anyone who witnessed the event could be confused as to what was happening (or what was *not* happening). Stanislaus Woywod offered the common-sense example of seminarians practicing the celebration of the Mass.[7] Woywod and others went so far as to say that, if it were obvious that one's imitation of the rites of Mass done out of derision or contempt for the Sacred Synaxis were pure mockery, such acts, though *more* grievously sinful than mere simulation, still would not constitute "simulation" in the canonical sense and would therefore not be punishable as a delict under canon 2322 of the 1917 Code.[8]

Moreover, several authors allowed for "pretense" in regard to a sacrament where such an act was undertaken to protect the good name of a member of the faithful. Dominicus Prümmer, for example, countenanced the making of the sign

5 See Ángel Marzoa, commenting on canon 1379 in A. Marzoa, et al., eds., *Exegetical Commentary on the Code of Canon Law*, in 5 vols. bound as 8, (Montreal: Wilson & Lafleur, 2004) IV/1, 504.

6 Felix Cappello, *Tractatus canonico-moralis de sacramentis iuxta Codicem juris canonici* [1921 et seq.], in 5 vols., 7° ed., (Marietti, 1962) I: 59, n. 66, wherein: "si quis communicaturo praebeat hostiam non consecratam pro consecrata ... in casu vera ac proprie dicta simulatio sacramenti nequaquam adest, sed solum *simulatio administrationis*, quae omnino differt a *simulatione confectionis*" (original emphasis).

7 Stanislaus Woywod, *A Practical Commentary on the Code of Canon Law* [1925], in 2 vols., rev. by C. Smith (Wagner/Herder, 1957) II, 521.

8 Ibid. See also Udalricus Beste, *Introductio in Codicem* [1938], 5th ed., (M. D'Auria Pontificius, 1961) 1032.

of the cross over a penitent to whom absolution was being refused—provided that the penitent knew that he was not being absolved—so as not to alert others that the penitent was being denied absolution.[9] But the practice at the shrine as outlined in your question differs markedly from these cases.

First, and most importantly, there is a high risk of deception of on-lookers at Mass insofar as the activity would look like a "Communion station" at which a chalice was being offered to recipients. Despite assurances to the contrary, it seems implausible that everyone at Mass knows that only grape juice is being administered from that particular chalice.[10] What would become of congregants who stepped into that line not knowing of the anomalous practice? Second, it is not clear that all of the recipients of this blessed grape juice fully understood that they were *not* receiving the Sacrament at this "Communion station." With the general grasp of basic Eucharistic doctrine at worrisome lows,[11] a such a practice cannot but help to foment confusion about a basic Church teaching. Third, of all possible simulations of a sacrament, simulation of *the Eucharist* is presented by commentators as being probably the worst simulation imaginable. One need only read canons 897[12] and 898[13] to understand why threats to the reverence due the Eucharist are viewed so strictly under law. From Slater to Marzoa,[14] distributing

9 Dominicus Prümmer, *Handbook of Moral Theology* [1921], 5° ed., Shelton trans., (Mercier, 1956) n. 544, 249. See also Thomas Slater, *A Manual of Moral Theology for English-Speaking Countries*, in 2 vols., 3rd ed., (Benziger, 1908) II, 40.

10 Aloysius Sabetti considered the scenario whereby, even though actual recipients of a non-consecrated host know that it is not owed adoration, mere observers of what appears to be the administration of the Sacred Species might be led into material idolatry. He therefore rejected as grievously sinful such administration of pseudo-Communion. Aloysius Sabetti, *Compendium Theologiae Moralis*, 4th ed. rev. by T. Barrett, (Pustet, 1924) n. 66, 560-561. Thus, what was considered gravely sinful, but non-criminal, under the 1917 Code, is, I suggest, now criminal under the 1983 Code.

11 Depending on the demographic group studied, belief in the Real Presence (*CCC* 1374) among American Catholics ranges from a high of (only) 90% to an astounding low of 40%. See Center for Applied Research in the Apostolate, "Sacraments Today: Belief and Practice among U. S. Catholics" (April, 2008), esp. "The Mass and the Eucharist" on-line at: http://cara.georgetown.edu/masseucharist.pdf.

12 Canon 897: "The most august sacrament is the Most Holy Eucharist in which Christ the Lord himself is contained, offered, and received and by which the Church continually lives and grows. The eucharistic sacrifice, the memorial of the death and resurrection of the Lord, in which the sacrifice of the cross is perpetuated through the ages is the summit and source of all worship and Christian life, which signifies and effects the unity of the People of God and brings about the building up of the body of Christ. Indeed, the other sacraments and all the ecclesiastical works of the apostolate are closely connected with the Most Holy Eucharist and ordered to it."

13 Canon 898: "The Christian faithful are to hold the Most Holy Eucharist in highest honor, taking an active part in the celebration of the most august sacrifice, receiving this sacrament most devoutly and frequently, and worshiping it with the highest adoration. In explaining the doctrine about this sacrament, pastors of souls are to teach the faithful diligently about this obligation."

14 Slater, 40; Marzoa, 504.

unconsecrated hosts is the prime example of simulation in the administration of sacraments.

The local ordinary of the shrine's territory has authority to investigate this practice (cc. 392, 1412), to order its immediate cessation, and further, to consider penal action in accord with canon 1341.[15] Thomas Green's observation should be recalled, namely, that canon 1379's call for a "just penalty" in response to simulation under canon 1379 suggests that this form of simulation is less serious than those forms of simulation penalized under canon 1378.[16]

But, that these other forms of simulation are penalized at all, and by a preceptive rather than a merely facultative penalty, suggests that *any* simulation in regard to a sacrament is a serious disturbance of the faith community. Support for this observation is found in the legislative history of canon 1379. The original draft of what eventually became canon 1379 read as follows: "Qui, ad malum finem praeter casus, de quibus in can. [1378], sacramentum se administrare simulat, iusta poena puniatur."[17] The phrase *ad malum finem* was *removed* from the proposed canon by the time of the 1980 *Schema Codicis*.[18] By removing the phrase *ad malum finem* from the provision, the motive of the simulator was eliminated as an element of the offense, although the official reason offered for the removal was based on the view of a consultor to the *Coetus de IurePoenali* that the phrase *ad malum finem* was redundant because "if *dolus* is present, the end will always be evil."[19]

This observation is not necessarily wrong, but it misses an important point. There are situations in which one might commit simulation of a sacrament in pursuit of a good end. Expanding on observations by Cappello, for example, we might posit a scenario in which a priest is tempted to simulate confection of the Eucharist where his life is in danger if he does not provide malefactors with the Eucharist for their sacrilegious purposes, and yet he anticipates their desecra-

15 Canon 1341: "An ordinary is to take care to initiate a judicial or administrative process to impose or declare penalties only after he has ascertained that fraternal correction or rebuke or other means of pastoral solicitude cannot sufficiently repair the scandal, restore justice, reform the offender."

16 Green, commenting on Canon 1379, in J. Coriden, et al., eds., *The Code of Canon Law: A Text and Commentary* (New York/Mahwah: Paulist Press, 1985) 925.

17 See Edward Peters, *Incrementa in Progressu 1983 Codicis Iuris Canonici* (Montreal: Wilson & Lafleur, 2005) 1188, *sub* Sanctionibus 56.

18 Ibid., *sub* 1980 *Schema Codicis* 1331.

19 In the unidentified consultor's words, "verba *ad malum finem* supprimi posse quia, si adest dolus, semper finis erit malus" *Communicationes* 9 (1977) 310.

tion of the Eucharist if he complies with their demand.[20] The unfortunate priest simulates confection of the species not only to save his own life but at the same time to render materially impossible the desecration of the Sacred Species. Such a ruse, however, we may say with Cappello, despite its good motives, would be forbidden as an act of simulation.[21] By its very nature, simulating the celebration or administration of a sacrament, as an abuse of a sacred thing, is always forbidden.[22]

Removal of the phrase *ad malum finem* from what became canon 1379, whether for the proffered reason or otherwise, prevented introducing confusion into the canonical tradition that the simulation of a sacrament, regardless of motive, is *always* an objective offense against the sacraments and admits of no excuse. That the shrine staff felt that offering grape juice to alcoholics was an inclusive gesture may be granted as a *moral* matter.[23] Moreover, should the case develop formally, their motives for simulating administration of the Eucharist would be relevant under canon 1344, nn. 2-3 in regard to punishment for their delict, but, of themselves, benign motives do not free offenders from culpability for having simulated the administration of any sacrament, especially the Eucharist.

As I said earlier, however, it is entirely possible that the practice you describe, though quite wrong, arose 'innocently enough' and that it will cease promptly once its wrongness is pointed out to shrine authorities.

Dr. Edward N. Peters, JD, JCD, Ref. Sig. Ap.

---

20 Cappello, I: 59, n. 66.

21 Ibid. For similar examples, see Eduardus Genicot & Ioseph Salsmans, *Casus conscientiae propositi et soluti*, 8° ed., (Uitgeverij, 1947), Casus 593, 422; or ArthurusVermeersch, *Theologiae Moralis: Principia, Responsa, Consilia* [1922], in 3 vols., 4° ed., (Rome: Gregorianum, 1947) III: 152-153; each rejecting the offering of non-consecrated hosts to sinners even in an attempt to prevent sacrilege.

22 Cappello, I: 59, n. 66: "Haberetur enim inductio ad materialem idololatriam, quam esse intrinsece malam ideoque semper illicitam, compertissimum est." See also P. Palazzini, ed., *Dictionarium Morale et Canonicum*, in 4 vols. (Rome: Officium Libri Catholici, 1962-1968) IV: 302-304, 302, s.v. "Simulatio."

23 Given the objective gravity of the practice, I think those involved in this scheme should go to Confession.

Canon 1481

The Appointment of an Advocate and the Bishop's Approval

An accused priest has submitted his mandate appointing a canonist whom he has chosen to be his canonical advocate. The Bishop had given the priest a list of "approved" canonists from which to choose his advocate. The advocate chosen by the priest was not on that list. The Bishop refused to approve the chosen advocate. Can the Bishop's disapproval over-ride the priest's right to choose his own advocate?

Opinion

The section of the 1983 Code of Canon Law dealing with procurators and advocates begins with the declaration of a canonical *right:* "A party can freely appoint his own advocate and procurator."[1] The Code of Canon Law gives to no one else except the priest-party in this case the *right* to appoint his advocate, and to exercise that right "freely."

Canon 1481 §2 requires that in a penal trial the accused must always have an advocate, either personally appointed by the accused himself, or assigned ("*datum*") by the judge.[2] Canon 1481 §3 requires that in a contentious trial concerning minors or the public good, the judge is to appoint an advocate for a party who does not have one.[3] While canon 1481 §1 confers on the accused priest the *right* to appoint his own advocate, canon 1481 §§2-3 confer on the judge – not on the Bishop – a conditional *duty* to appoint an advocate in two limited circumstances. This duty arises in trials in which the law itself mandates that the accused, or the party-defendant, have an advocate, and the accused party or defendant has not appointed his own advocate and is, therefore, without an advocate.

The "either…or" phrases of canon 1481 §2, "…an advocate *either* appointed personally by the accused, *or* assigned to him by the judge, are not a basis for inferring that the accused and the judge have equal authority to appoint an advo-

1 Canon 1481 §1: "*Pars libere potest advocatum et procuratorem sibi constituere.*"

2 Canon 1481 §2: "*In iudicio poenali accusatus aut a se constitutum aut a iudice datum, semper habere debet advocatum.*"

3 Canon 1481 §3: "*In iudicio contentioso, si agatur de minoribus aut de iudicio in quo bonum publicum vertitur, exceptis causis matrimonialibus, iudex parti carenti defensorem ex officio constituat.*"

cate for the accused. To understand the meaning of the "or" phrase, "*aut a iudice datum,*" one must read it in conjunction with canon 1723 which deals explicitly with how the requirement of an advocate in a penal trial is to be fulfilled.

Canon 1723 §1[4] requires a judge "to invite the accused to appoint an advocate for himself, in accordance with canon 1481, §1." If the accused does not do so, a *duty* devolves upon the judge to appoint an advocate for the accused.[5] In other words, the judge has no *right* to appoint the accused priest's advocate, but does have a duty to do so when the law requires an advocate and the priest has not appointed his own advocate. Even then, the advocate appointed by the judge can serve as the accused priest's advocate only until the priest appoints an advocate of his own choice. "The advocate appointed *ex officio* is replaced automatically if and when the accused priest himself appoints one, freely using his right to choose a defense counsel."[6] This canon confirms the exclusive right of a priest-party to appoint his own advocate. No one can interfere with the exercise of that right. It is to be exercised "freely," and it is not subservient to anyone else's wishes.

Although the priest is free to choose any advocate and procurator he wishes, the advocate and procurator he chooses must fulfill the requirements of canon law for such offices. Canon 1483 requires both the advocate and the procurator to have attained the age of majority and be of good repute. In addition, the canon requires that an advocate, but not a procurator, be a Catholic, unless the diocesan bishop permits otherwise, and have a doctorate in canon law, or be otherwise truly expert ("*peritus*") and "be approved by the same diocesan bishop."[7]

Canon 1657of the 1917 code[8] gave the then-qualifications for procurators and advocates, but made no mention of a need for the diocesan bishop's approval

---

4 Canon 1723 §1: "Iudex reum citans debet eum invitare ad advocatum, ad norman can. 1481, §1, intra terminum ab ipso iudice praefinitum, sibi constituendum."

5 Canon 1723 §2: "Quod si reus non providerit, iudex ante litis contestationem advocatum ipse nominet, tamdiu in munere mansurum quamdiu reus sibi advocatum non constituerit."

6 *Code of Canon Law Annotated*, 2nd Ed., Ernest Caparros, Helene Aube (Montreal: Wilson & Lafleur Limitee, 2004) 1351.

7 Canon 1483: "Procurator et advocatus esse debent aetate maiores et bonae famae; advocatus debet praeterea esse catholicus, nisi Episcopus diocesanus aliter permittat, et doctor in iure canonico, vel alioquin vere peritus et ab eodem Episcopus approbatus." Canon 1657 §2 of *CIC*/17 stated that the advocate had to be a doctor of canon law or "someone truly expert, *at least in canon law*" ("*saltem in iure canonico*"). Canon 1483 of *CIC* 1983 does not contain the last phrase "at least in canon law," although it would be reasonable to assume that being well qualified to serve as an advocate would entail having a good grasp of canon law, in accord with which the advocate is to advise his client and present his client's case.

8 1917 *CIC* c. 1657 §1: "Procurator et advocatus esse debent catholici, aetate maiores, bonae famae; acatholicus non admittitur, nisi per exceptionem et ex necessitate. 1917 *CIC* c. 1657 §2: "Advocatus debet praeterea esse doctor vel alioqui vere peritus, saltem in iure canonico."

being necessary for either office. A separate canon (1917 *CIC* c. 1658),[9] however, treated of the need for the bishop's approval, stating that the procurator "needs no prior approval by the Ordinary as long as he fulfills the requirements given in the preceding canon. In order to be admitted to the office of advocate, however, the advocate needs the approval of the Ordinary."[10] This separate treatment in the 1917 Code of "qualifications" and "approval" indicated that these are different concepts: "approval" is not one of the qualifications; it means something entirely different.

The 1983 Code bundled these two canons into one canon, canon 1483, which treats both "qualifications" and "approval" together. After giving the two qualifications necessary for procurators and advocates (age of reason and good reputation), the canon gives two additional qualifications necessary for an advocate (Catholicity unless the diocesan bishops permits otherwise, and a doctorate or expertise in canon law) and finishes with the phrase "and approved by the same bishop." On what grounds can a bishop's approval be withheld?[11]

Being qualified and being approved are two different concepts. The bishop's approval or disapproval of an otherwise qualified advocate cannot be subjective or arbitrary, for this would be tantamount to giving the bishop canonical authority to violate the priest's right to *freely appoint* his own advocate. The bishop's disapproval can only be based on an objective finding by the bishop that the proposed advocate lacks one or more of the four qualifications listed in canon 1483, and is, therefore, not qualified.

The bishop has the power of governance in his diocese, which includes seeing that those who hold ecclesiastical offices in his diocese, including advocates, are qualified. In 1923, the Signatura decided against some advocates who claimed that, because they were admitted to practice before the Roman Curia, they could practice in any diocesan tribunal without the approval of the local bishop. The decision was based on the power of governance given by law to bishops in their own dioceses, a power "limited only by the general laws of the Church...."[12]

9 1917 *CIC* c. 1658 §2: "Advocatus autem, ut ad patrocinium admittatur, indigent approbatione Ordinarii, quae aut generalis sit ad omnes causas aut specialis pro certa causa." The term Ordinary includes diocesan bishops. (cf. 1917 *CIC* c. 198).

10 A procurator is one who is appointed by the party to act in his stead, if the party chooses not to act for himself. He is the party's *alter ego*. A party can have only one procurator. An advocate is more literally the party's lawyer. He advises the accused on canon law, prepares legal documents, proposes questions for witnesses (canon 1561), presents and argues the case for his client. A party can have one or several advocates.

11 Canon 1658 of the 1917 code also stated that no prior approval is necessary for a procurator.

12 Cf. "Canon 335" in *Canon Law Digest*, Vol. I, p. 199.

In other words, it is the duty of the local bishop to pass on the qualifications of advocates practicing in his own diocese, no matter where else they have been approved to practice. If the bishop finds that the advocate proposed by the priest has attained the age of maturity, has a good reputation, is a Catholic[13], and is either a doctor of canon law or one who is otherwise an expert or well versed in canon law, the bishop must approve him. The essential qualification for an advocate is that he be a doctor of canon law or otherwise be an expert, one well versed in canon law, for it is on canon law that the advocate is to advise his client, and according to which he must prosecute his clients rights. The general law of the Church today is that an accused has the right to freely appoint his own advocate, and that a bishop has an affirmative duty to protect the rights of his priests, "*eorum iura tutetur*" (c. 384). The refusal to approve a qualified advocate chosen by the accused priest would violate those laws.

The ordinary has a duty to facilitate the exercise of the priest's right, and not interfere with it. The existence of a list of advocates whom the bishop may have pre-approved can in no way limit the priest's right to "freely appoint" his own advocate. Any such attempted limitation on the exercise of that right is an infringement of that right. The conclusion that a diocesan bishop must approve a qualified expert chosen by the accused priest seems ineluctable.

Sacramentorum sanctitatis tutela, Art. 11, requires a doctorate in canon law for one to serve as an advocate in cases reserved to the CDF, which include those alleging the sexual abuse of a minor by a cleric. The CDF can, however, dispense from this requirement, but only for those who have a licentiate in canon law and who have worked in ecclesiastical tribunals for a reasonable time. Art. 12 provides that only priests can validly serve as procurators and advocates, but the CDF can also dispense from the requirement of priesthood. It is the practice of the CDF to grant either or both of these dispensations if the Ordinary who submits a case to the CDF requests them. Given the priest's canonical right to appoint his own advocate and his bishop's obligation to protect that right, it follows that the bishop would have an obligation to petition the CDF for those dispensations if needed. The Ordinary could properly ask the CDF for a dispensation from a doctorate in canon law only if he had first assured himself that the proposed advocate fulfills all of the CDF's requirements for advocacy. The request to the CDF for a dispensation would naturally presume this finding.

Canon 1481 §1 does not limit a priest's right to freely appoint a procurator and an advocate solely in penal or contentious trials. Nothing prevents a priest from

13 Canon 1483 gives the bishop the authority to allow a non-catholic as well.

appointing and acting through a procurator-advocate for any matter for which he feels he may need canonical services.[14] Any matter involving a priest's personal and canonical rights would warrant his obtaining canonical representation. The following readily come to mind: administrative procedures; the issuance of personal decrees or precepts against him; being informed of an allegation of sexual abuse of a minor brought against him; the initiation of a canon 1717 preliminary investigation; a canonical procedure initiated against him to remove him from his pastoral office; generally any dispute that might arise with his superior or possibly subject him to penalties or disciplinary action. Furthermore, the law permits a priest to speak for himself or to do so through a procurator. If a priest chooses to appoint and speak through a procurator, a diocesan bishop should abide by the priest's wishes, and would seemingly be obliged to deal with the priest's canonical procurator.

In summary: Only an objective finding that a proposed advocate lacks one or more of the qualifications prescribed by law for an advocate, can justify the withholding of a diocesan bishop's approval of the advocate chosen by the accused priest. A bishop's refusal to approve an advocate simply because the advocate is not on an "approved list" of advocates predetermined by the bishop is a violation of canon 1481 §1.

Dr. Charles Renati, JCD, JD

14 The same person can be appointed to serve as both procurator and advocate.

Canon 1486-1487

Procedure to Remove a Procurator or Advocate

Recently, a tribunal officer explained that a procurator wished to withdraw his mandate but the respondent who had legitimately nominated him refused later to communicate with the tribunal. The question was raised if there is another possibility for the procurator to withdraw his mandate, and if so, what process would be followed?

Opinion

Canons 1486-1487 of the 1983 Code of Canon Law and articles 108-109 *Dignitas connubii* are the norms to be followed.

Canon 1486 §1 states that for the removal of a procurator or advocate to take effect, they must be informed. The first part of paragraph one refers to the procedure to be followed for the removal of a legal representative *before* the joinder of issues. The main issue is that the party who legitimately nominated someone as procurator (advocate) in a case withdraws the mandate. The canon does not speak directly of the possibility for a party to renounce the mandate of his/her procurator (advocate); this possibility is simply assumed in the norm. Furthermore, the tribunal has no influence on the free choice of a procurator (advocate) or its removal from the cause according to canon 1486. It is simply sufficient that the party informs the procurator (advocate) about the removal; no mention is made concerning the tribunal, the other party, etc. Furthermore, no grave cause is required by law for this type of removal.

It would seem appropriate for the norm to require in this case also that the tribunal be informed of the removal since the tribunal has only the legitimate mandate of the procurator (advocate) and difficulties can arise when the tribunal proceeds without knowing that the procurator has no legitimate mandate. This may have an important impact on the cause, since all these acts are considered invalid if a procurator lacks a legitimate mandate: e.g., in a marriage nullity cause if the procurator without legitimate mandate introduces new grounds before the joinder of issues; in an ordinary contentious trial if same procurator introduces a counterclaim before the joinder of issues; etc.

The second part of canon 1486 §1 requires that, for the removal of a procurator (advocate) *after* the joinder of issues, the legal representative, the judge, and the opposing party are to be informed. Again, the law focuses on the desire of a party to remove a legitimately appointed procurator (advocate), and no grave cause is required by law for this type of removal.

Thus, canon 1486 §1 addresses simply the situation in which a party withdraws the mandate of a legitimately appointed procurator (advocate), whether before or after the joinder of issues. No grave cause for its removal is required in either situation. The provision of article 108 *Dignitas connubii* is basically the same as the provision of canon 1486 §1, but the former includes the condition "without prejudice to the obligation of paying the remuneration due them for the work they have done."

Canon 1486 §2 states that the right and duty to appeal after the definitive sentence remains with the procurator if the mandating party does not refuse. This provision does not deal with the removal of the mandate of a legitimately appointed procurator and would more appropriately appear as a part of canon 1485. *Dignitas connubii* made this correction by transferring the provision of canon 1486 §2 to article 107 (the equivalent of canon 1485) as its paragraph 2.

Canon 1487 (as well as article 109 of *Dignitas connubii*) states that, for a grave cause, the judge, either *ex officio* or at the request of a party, can remove the procurator (advocate) by a decree. In this case it is the judge who can remove a proposed procurator (advocate) for a grave cause. This norm uses the term *gravi tamen de causa* without further explanation. It is left to the judge to decide what is a possible "grave cause" to remove a procurator (advocate). This leaves much room for discretion, but the judge must not act recklessly. Reasons for removal may result from inappropriate behavior by the legal representative, lack of suitability, personal interest in the cause, or doubts in the procedural capacity of the procurator, etc.

Furthermore, "a party" (*ad instantiam partis*), including the opposing party, can submit a request for removal. A legitimate reason for such a request might be the fact that the party's relationship with the procurator (advocate) could reasonably impair the objective character of the cause. (One should note, however, that the promoter of justice and the defender of the bond are not considered "parties" in the cause according to canon 1434, 2°.)

The original question posed was whether or not a procurator has a way of personally withdrawing his/her mandate. According to the German canonist Joseph Weier, the code lacks several provisions concerning the mandate: there is no precise provision concerning the duration of a legitimate mandate, concerning its expiration upon termination of the litigation, and concerning the ability of the procurator (advocate) to withdraw the mandate personally.[1]

A brief look into the drafting period shows that this option was actually discussed. Canon 98 §3 of the *Schema de processibus* stated: "Advocati et procuratores vetantur renunciare mandato, lite pendente, nisi iusta de causa, a tribunali probanda."[2] The consultors voted unanimously that this provision is superfluous.[3]

Based on this drafting history, one might conclude that a legitimately appointed procurator cannot withdraw his/her mandate personally. There is no legal foundation in the 1983 code or *Dignitas connubii.* The legitimately appointed procurator is to fulfill his/her function, and his/her mandate can only be revoked by request of the party or, for a grave cause, by the judge at the request of the opposing party or *ex officio*, as a result of misconduct or abuse of office.

The question whether or not a procurator can withdraw personally from his/her function depends on the interpretation of *superflua* (superfluous) as used by the consultors during the drafting period.

It can be interpreted to mean that the consultors thought it is so obvious that a procurator can renounce personally his/her function at any stage of the trial that there is no need to have it as additional norm in the code. But if this is the case, to whom does the procurator direct his/her withdrawal to be legitimate? Is there any difference if he/she withdraws from the function before or after the joinder of issues – similar to canon 1486 §1?

Another possible interpretation could be that the consultors thought this case actually would never happen in practice, so that basically once someone is appointed procurator, there is no need for him/her to withdraw from the office unless he/she asks the party to remove him/her from the function.

Whether a procurator could withdraw his/her function personally in a cause seems to be a *lacuna* in the law. Since this possibility was considered superfluous and eliminated in the drafting period without any further explanation, it would be reasonable to conclude that, with reference to similar possibilities, a legitimately nominated procurator can withdraw his/her function personally at any stage of

1 J. Weier, "Der Anwaltimkirchlichen Eheprozeß. Neue Bestimmungenim CIC," in A. Gabriels and H. J. F. Reinhardt (eds.), *Ministerium Iustitiae. Festschrift für Heribert Heinemann zur Vollendung des 60.Lebensjahres* (Ludgerus Verlag, Essen, 1986) 409.

2 *Communicationes* 10 [1978] 271.

3 "Suggestum est ut deleatur §3 quae videtur superflua (placet omnibus)." Ibid., 272.

the process by informing the party he/she represents, the opposing party, and the tribunal. A grave cause for the withdrawal might not be required.[4]

Dr. Michael Nobel, JCD

4 Despite the *lacuna*, some guidance might be found in the norms of canons 187-190 on resignation from office.

Contributors

Rev. Brendan Daly, JCD is Principal of Good Shepherd College in Auckland, New Zealand and Associate Judicial Vicar in the Regional Tribunal of New Zealand.

Rev. John F. Doerfler, STD, JCL is Vicar General and Chancellor in the Diocese of Green Bay, Wisconsin.

Dr. Chad J. Glendinning, JCD is an Assistant Professor of Canon Law at Saint Paul University, Ottawa, Ontario, Canada.

Sr. Amy Hereford, CSJ, JD, JCL works as an attorney and canonist with CSJ Ministries, consulting with religious institutes on a variety of legal matters and facilitating chapters of discernment.

Sr. Sharon L. Holland, IHM, JCD is Vice-President of the Sister Servants of the Immaculate Heart of Mary, Monroe, Michigan and a canonical consultant to Religious Institutes.

Dr. John M. Huels, JCD is a Professor of Canon Law at Saint Paul University, Ottawa, Canada.

Dr. Eileen C. Jaramillo, JCL, DMin serves as a canonical consultant for women religious. She is also a judge for the Diocese of Lansing, Michigan and Adjunct Faculty, Siena Heights University and Ecumenical Theological Seminary.

Mrs. Daniela S. Knepper, JCL is Defender of the Bond for the Diocese of Phoenix.

Dr. Michael Nobel, JCD is an Assistant Professor of Canon Law at Saint Paul University, Ottawa, Ontario, Canada.

Dr. Edward N. Peters, JD, JCD, Ref. Sig. Ap. holds the Edmund Cardinal Szoka Chair at Sacred Heart Major Seminary in Detroit, Michigan, and is a Referendary of the Apostolic Signatura.

Dr. Charles G. Renati, JCD, JD is in private canon and civil law practice, San Francisco, California.

Msgr. John A. Renken STD, JCD is a Professor of Canon Law at Saint Paul University, Ottawa, Ontario, Canada.

Ms. Amy Strickland, JCL is Associate Director for Canon Law at the Resource Center for Religious Institutes in Silver Spring, Maryland.

Sr. Victoria Vondenberger, RSM, JCL is the coordinator of a group of ten men and women religious who are also canonists willing to consult about religious life issues. This opinion represents the views and experiences of all the members of the group.